Praise for *Vision: The Blueprint for Life-Building*

Vision is an inspiring, biblically grounded, practical guide to Vision Boarding for the Christian woman. I highly recommend this book for Christian coaches working with women hungry to discover and live out their unique God-given vision.

SUSAN BORGSTROM, MA, ACC, CCC
Director, Awakening in Nature, NFP

Rooted in biblical stories and rich with life wisdom, *Vision: The Blueprint for Life Building* by Julie Stroud, will help readers, especially those who feel lost or stuck, listen for God's call. Stroud tells familiar biblical stories in fresh new ways and shares her experience and expertise to help readers find their own blueprint for life.

ROCHELLE MELANDER, WRITENOWCOACH.COM
Professional Coach and Author of Write-A-Thon:
Write Your Book in 26 Days (And Live to Tell About It)

Vision: The Blueprint for Life-Building provides the reader with a powerful combination of rich Bible study, clear theology, relevant historical context, and compelling contemporary stories of how God continues to lead and work today. Julie writes with humility, vulnerability, and great compassion, and she finishes each chapter with thought-provoking questions that will help you hone in on God's vision for your own life.

KELLI WORRALL
Speaker and Author of *Pierced and Embraced:*
7 Life-Changing Encounters with the Love of Christ

D1276816

An excellent coach [who's lived these truths], Julie Stroud deftly and joyfully invites us into the possibilities of becoming who God sees us to be. Affirming and easily applicable, *Vision: The Blueprint for Life-Building* offers a biblical blueprint for seeing and building that life.

JANE RUBIETTA
Speaker, Coach, and Author of 20 books, including
Worry Less, Live More and *Finding Your Dream*

Vision is an inspiring and thought-provoking book for any leader who wishes to learn how to live by vision. Stroud provides the biblical framework and practical tools needed to help us lead lives of purpose.

MONA BOELENS, MPA
Executive Director, Kindred Life Ministries

Having a clear and ambitious vision for the future has been key to my ability to juggle so much, to stay the course during tough times and to achieve goals. Julie Stroud is a born visionary and a generous coach who has tapped into a thought-provoking way to explore our collective desire to create lives filled with meaning and connection. This book will surely change lives.

KATE COLBERT
Communications Consultant, Speaker, and Author of
*Think Like a Marketer: How a Shift in Mindset
Can Change Everything for Your Business*

VISION

The Blueprint for Life Building

VISION

The Blueprint for Life Building

Bob —
1st Thes. 5:24 !!
Thanks for the interview.
In Him, Julie Stroud

JULIE STROUD

FERVENT
coaching

Vision: The Blueprint for Life-Building

©2018 Julie Stroud

Published by Silver Tree Publishing

Note: All stories contained within are true, although some names have been changed.

Library of Congress Control Number: 2018954305

To my sons—I always knew I wanted to be a mother. Now you are building your lives. As you look ahead, I pray you live by vision and know the deep satisfaction of following God. You'll find your treasure there.

To all who generously shared your stories, thank you.

To my friends who prayed along with me throughout this project, thank you.

Last, and certainly not least, thank you, Lord, for doing a work in me.

To the dreamers and the doers
and for anyone who sincerely seeks the heart of God,
this book is for you.

Contents

1

The Kitchen Sink

Gray afternoon scenery matched the lulling activity of washing the same dishes I'd washed a thousand times before. As I noticed winter waning and branches budding, I plotted my monthly sales progress. Washing dishes, looking out the window, adding numbers, and estimating goals. This was my daily rinse, wash, repeat. Only today, I injected an exciting variation.

The year was 2002. I was mother to two little boys and a sales rep for a kitchenware direct sales company. Every afternoon, I'd put the kids down for naps, take a few minutes to tidy the kitchen, then work at my desk for an hour. My inner dialogue included estimating remaining sales for the month, tracking my progress toward bigger incentives, and jotting lists of calls to make. Another component of the business involved recruiting and training new reps. That afternoon, I felt a restlessness with the same old, same old.

"Lord, somewhere out there today is another woman standing at her kitchen sink, washing her dishes. Just like me, she's thinking about her life and areas for improvement. Perhaps being a sales rep on my team is the answer to her prayers. Will you cross our paths?"

I could picture her and imagine her thoughts.

I continued, "Lord, send me someone to help. A Christian woman also raising little kids. A woman who could be a new friend." I could sense the vision growing more clearly, and I wasn't done yet. "Lord, I love the name Cami. Can you send me a Cami to join my team?"

I'm a traditional evangelical believer. I don't have the spiritual gifts of prophecy or speaking in tongues. Up to that moment, the prayers I had prayed for my business were general in nature. That day's specific prayer was surprising—and a little fun.

A few days later, I got a phone call.

"Hello ... my friend attended a party, liked your products, and gave me your number. I've been looking for a part-time opportunity to work around my family." This is a rare call to receive in the direct sales business.

"Sure," I replied. "I'd love to tell you about it. What's your name?" My jaw dropped when she answered, "Cami."

She proceeded to explain that her family had recently moved to the area for her husband's assignment at the local navy base. They settled in and found a great Bible-believing church to attend. And she homeschooled her two young sons. This woman could become my newest friend. I was glowing.

So I went back to the Lord in prayer, laughing at this Cami encounter. "Lord, you truly care about the details of our lives! Can I ask for another person to help? Dare I ask for more? I like the name Katie and I don't have any Katies on my team. Do you have a woman named Katie I can help?"

A consistent salesperson, I conducted six parties a month and achieved most of the incentives my direct sales company offered. I had sponsored many people in the past but didn't always enjoy the process. These new prayers shifted my sponsoring efforts toward serving others.

Within a few nights, I was selling my wares at another home party. When we went around the room with introductions, I had to hold back when the woman directly across from me said, "My name is Katie."

I smiled—perhaps too enthusiastically—and asked, "How do you spell your name?" I wanted to jump up and down when she confirmed, "K-A-T-I-E."

I proceeded with my presentation, perhaps a little more upbeat than usual. When it was over, Katie approached me and asked questions about the business. "Is it hard to get parties? How many hours a week do you do this?"

"You're curious about this?" I asked. "I noticed you watched everything I did up there!" Within a week, she was my newest team member.

Of course, I returned to my prayers, praising God and laughing. "This is so strange and fun and almost unreal, God! You are so good to me, and Cami and Katie. Lord, can I ask … Katie is a common name. Is there another Katie, or Kathy, or Kathryn you would like me to meet?"

Two parties later, a single young woman named Kathleen was in attendance. She asked me, "Is it possible to make some decent side money doing this? I just bought my first place and I would like the funds to decorate it now." She became the next representative on my sales team.

This is not a joke! This is a true story. What an exciting burst of extraordinary sponsoring activity. I wish I could say I continued sponsoring scores of sales reps with this mindset and method. I wish I could say my sales team swelled in size and we swept national sales goals. But I can't.

This freaked me out just a bit.

Could it be that my thoughts were powerful enough to bring about small things and even make my dreams come true? What about God's provision and will? Should I go after the things I want or let the Lord send blessings as He sees fit? How do I achieve what I believe I am capable of? Deeper still, how could I know that this business was my best option for serving God? With no shortage of questions, you could say I had a small crisis of faith.

I went back to the kitchen sink and the inner dialogue of sales goals and the stuff of life. Wash, rinse, repeat. It was safer to stick with business as usual and habits that were comfortable. It seemed I'd stumbled upon a purposeful, prayerful, and fun recruiting approach. Before I had the chance to fully test it for continued results, I stopped.

And I returned to believing that the way to achieve was blood, sweat, and tears. Earning promotions, incentives, and trips came through my hard work and dedication. Many times, I worked to the bitter end to achieve my short-term goals. Late nights, worrying, and nail-biting scenarios, I believed, were a part of a sales job.

A few years later, everyone was talking about the film *The Secret*. It taught a concept called the Law of Attraction and claimed our thoughts create our life. It claimed that turning our thoughts in the right direction sets right things in our path. I found the concept both fascinating and frightening.

Is this the key that unlocks the dream life or unleashes the devil of the self-governed life? Could this be the way to success … or the gnarly path to skewed Scripture?

I grew up in the church: Sunday school, children's choir, youth group, mission trips, a church-every-Sunday-kinda-girl. Despite this foundation, I did not receive Jesus as my personal Savior until I went away to college.

That first Sunday on campus, I slept in. In fact, I slept in and skipped church for eight straight weeks. Thank goodness it only took that short time to realize the fading echo of worship slipping from my soul. I faced my sinful propensity to be the master of my life and gave my heart to Christ. I asked the Lord to come in, dismantle my ugliness, and begin a reconstruction project in me. After years of trying to be good, I was being restored day by day and was finally free to truly worship Jesus as my Redeemer.

When *The Secret* came about, my storehouse of sermons stirred me to see it as false teaching. I believed that God cared about the details of our lives. On the other hand, asking God for everything but the kitchen sink seemed more like treating Him as a Santa Claus in the sky. I didn't want a shallow faith of God doing what I wanted. I wanted a bold faith following what *He* wanted.

By this point, I was the mother of three boys and segueing from direct sales leader to business coach. My sales team and my clients possessed stronger confidence and produced greater results using vision boards and visualizations. Since I had people looking to me for guidance, I needed to know we weren't playing with fire. If we were, we'd need to snuff it out. I wanted to understand how personal performance fit into God's plan. I committed to uncovering the truth.

This book is the culmination of my quest. It's also the kicking off point for a life vision drenched in a biblical mindset. In an attempt to reach our dreams and goals, we have a tendency to throw everything but the kitchen sink at it. Books, seminars, how-to steps, and teaching of all sorts seem appealing and helpful. We tend to complicate matters. What if we only needed the Word of God to live the life He has for us?

Identifying a good thing from a God thing requires "visioneering." As Andy Stanley put it, "Dreamers dream about things being different. Visionaries envision themselves making a difference."[1] This is the kind of vision shown throughout Scripture. We are God's workmanship, created in Christ for good works, which God prepared for us a long time ago.[2] We are a product of God's vision to be used for His greater purposes.

So it seems the Christian's task is to discover what it is that God designed for us to do. And then do it, like the Nike slogan says. We can move from vision boards of vacations and big paychecks. It's not that those things are unworthy in and of themselves. But a life focused on exciting accomplishments and accouterments is similar to a story filled with exclamation points or a buffet of chocolate cakes and pastries. It winds up being the pursuit of hollow things. No substance. We can think bigger, broader, longer, and deeper.

---

[1] Andy Stanley, *Visioneering* (Colorado Springs: Multnomah, 2016), 34.
[2] Ephesians 2:10, paraphrased.

A life saved by God and lived for God shines for God. Dare to envision a life shining like a star against His sky of wide and long and high and deep love.

QUESTIONS FOR REFLECTION

- Recall an instance when my dreams materialized. To what do I attribute that experience—the vision in my mind's eye, my hard work, God's blessing, or a combination of things?

- People with vision imagine making a difference. What difference do I want to make?

- A life saved by God and lived for God shines for God. How does this statement strike me? Has my life been transformed by Jesus Christ? Am I living for God? Is my testimony evident? Am I authentic in these areas?

2

Wish upon a Star and Set Sail

Vision, Miracles, and God's Will

Who hasn't gazed at the sky on a clear night and wished upon a star? The first recorded experience of this very thing is in Genesis when God directed an elderly and childless Abraham outside. God said, "Look up at the sky and count the stars—if indeed you can count them." Then he said to him, "So shall your offspring be."[1] Wish upon a star, and your wildest dreams will come true.

I grew up the youngest of four girls to parents who lived through the Depression, so we didn't dream much. My parents came from very little. My mom's childhood included moving to a cheaper apartment each spring when the lease was up and the landlord raised the rent. My dad started working at the age of nine as a pin setter at the local bowling alley. When he got paid, he brought his earnings directly to his mom to help her pay the bills.

---

[1] 15:5.

No wonder when my parents met and married, their dream was financial security. They raised us girls with the values of responsibility, hard work, and practical decision-making. We were expected to go to college and pursue a career and a steady paycheck.

Couple that with our traditional Christian experience. We went to church every Sunday and prayed at dinner and bedtime. I learned Bible stories in Sunday school. And that's exactly how I understood these vignettes—*as stories*. I could not imagine Scripture as literal and historical fact, nor could I understand God's Word as actual promises that would come to pass.

After becoming a believer as a young adult, I read familiar passages with fresh eyes. No longer did I doubt Scripture's accuracy and application; I personally knew the Lord's love and leadership. I no longer felt directionless; I was heaven bound.

ABRAHAM'S STORY

The story of Abraham begins in the Mesopotamian city of Ur. Although his family descended from Noah, Abraham's father followed the culture and worshipped idols. As was the custom, Abraham stayed near his family until his father's passing.

Then God told him, "Go from your country, your people and your father's household to the land I will show you. I will make you into a great nation, and I will bless you; I will make your name great, and you will be a blessing."[2]

Like Noah, when God spoke, Abraham obeyed. This could be considered crazy; after all, Abraham was seventy-five and childless. When Abraham arrived in Canaan, God told him that his descendants would inherit the land. Abraham built an altar there to mark God's promises.

As the story unfolds, Abraham's faults are revealed. When famine forced the family to relocate to Egypt, Abraham told his beautiful wife, Sarah, that he would lie if need be. Fearing

---

[2] 12:1–2.

he would be killed so the Egyptians could easily take Sarah for their own, Abraham planned to pass her off as his sister. He did not count on Sarah being sent off as Pharaoh's concubine. As her supposed brother, Abraham was rewarded with a dowry of sheep and cattle.

The Lord came to King Abimelek in a dream and told him the truth about Sarah and Abraham. The king had been set up, and he was angry. Rather than anger God, in a fit of rage Abimelek sent them away.

Abraham left wealthier with his livestock.

The experience in Egypt revealed Abraham as an everyday man and a product of his culture. He followed God most of the time, and other times went his own way.

God visited Abraham again and reminded him that all the land he saw was for him and his offspring. "I will make your offspring like the dust of the earth, so that if anyone could count the dust, then your offspring could be counted."[3] Still no children in sight, so why did God continue to bring this up?

In His infinite wisdom and longsuffering patience, God came to Abraham in a vision once again. "Do not be afraid, Abram. I am your shield, your very great reward."

But doubt rolled in and Abraham questioned God.

"I think you mean Eliezer, my head servant. He will be my heir. Sarah and I still don't have any kids."

That's when God directed Abraham outside to gaze at the night sky. Not His first time making this promise, God was emphatic with Abraham. Here in chapter 15, God casts an unforgettable vision.

Look at the stars, Abraham! Do you understand now?

Amazingly, Abraham did not entirely understand. Or he did, and he was not patient. In biblical times, having children was paramount to life success, so Sarah took matters into her own hands. She insisted that Abraham have relations with her maidservant Hagar. A son any which way was better than none at all!

---

[3] 13:16.

9

At the age of eighty-six, Abraham became a father to Ishmael. However, this was not the blessing God envisioned. The nation of Israel was to come from the seed of Abraham and his wife, Sarah.

One more time God came in a vision to ninety-nine-year-old Abraham. The statement this time was, "Walk before me faithfully and be blameless." Abraham fell face down before the Lord, a sign of humility and worship. God went on to promise, "You will be the father of many nations."[4]

It was at this point that God renamed him from Abram (noble father), as he'd been known his whole life, to Abraham (father of many). Sarah got a new name, too, from Sarai (princess) to Sarah (mother of many). Their new names reflected the wisdom and maturity they had developed over time.

At long last, Abraham and Sarah conceived their one and only son, Isaac.

God appeared to Abraham no less than four times over a twenty-four-year period. Each time the message was the same—he would be the father of countless descendants. God sought and chose Abraham. This covenant was a God-directed one-way promise to make him fruitful with family.

During that twenty-four-year span, Abraham lived an authentic faith. From obeying God to doubting His plan, from cowardice in Egypt to consorting with his concubine, to finally falling facedown before the Lord, we see his spiritual growth. Abraham's preparation was his maturation, a necessity for the vision to unfold.

Abraham and Sarah are much like you and me. Sometimes we follow God wholeheartedly; other times we take matters into our own hands.

But God never gives up on us; He continues to make Himself known in big and small ways. He gives opportunity after opportunity to listen, to yield, to follow, and to grow into the man or woman God has seen all along.

---

[4] 17:1–6.

He looks long-range and sees our potential. We look at today and see our problems.

Interestingly, God's promise to Abraham expanded. God's original promise was to make Abraham into a great nation. By God's fourth visit, he claimed that Abraham would be the father of many nations. God spoke a bigger vision to a humbler man. From God's covenant to Abraham came blessing for countless people. From Abraham to Isaac to Jacob and his twelve sons came the twelve tribes of Israel.

The lesson here is clear: God did something *in* Abraham before he did something *through* Abraham. The same is true for us. God is a God of relationship and He wants to do a work in us before, during, and after He does some amazing work through us.

VISIONS IN BIBLICAL TIMES AND TODAY

God used visions in biblical times to reveal His plan and to place His people in prominent positions. Both Joseph and Daniel received visions from God and the ability to interpret dreams (visions are the same as dreams but happen at a different time: visions occur during waking hours; dreams occur during sleep). Both Joseph and Daniel rose to prominent positions and made an impact for God's kingdom. Joseph was at the right hand of Pharaoh during a time of famine, and his leadership saved Egypt from calamity. Daniel was number one advisor to King Darius, and because of his devotion to God, he won over King Darius and Babylon became a society open to religious expression. These are just two examples—there are many!

Visions such as these do not occur any longer. God came down, inserted Himself into humanity, and wrote His story for us. Believers today have the Bible, telling us everything we need to know. Salvation through Jesus Christ is made plain. The Bible is our traveler's guide. Believers today also have the Holy Spirit, the gift God gave upon Christ's ascension. The Holy Spirit is our internal compass, directing us to the true north of Scripture and a life of obedience.

The Greek word transliterated as *kanōn* (canon) in English means a straight rod or rule.[5] Early Christians referred to this as "rule of faith" or "rule of law." Hundreds of years ago, the Word of God was often interchanged with the common phrase "rule of faith."[6]

God's Word provides the measure by which we align our lives. The early Christian council established the canon, the sixty-six books of the Bible, by the third century. They used guidelines that included a requirement that New Testament books had to be linked to people who could give firsthand eyewitness accounts. Jude, the half brother of Jesus, wrote about "the faith that was once for all entrusted to God's holy people."[7]

Scholars conclude that this means that Scripture was given once for the benefit of all. The bottom line is this: *the canon is closed.* Any further visions do not add to theology or refine what has been done.

Visions we experience today are for the purpose of our sanctification in Christ and our personal walk with the Lord. Godly visions will never contradict Scripture or add to it—the Scripture is complete as it is. Furthermore, visions must line up with the Word. If a vision is not true, we must dismiss it.

Visions today are often described as a dream, an inspiration, or a nudge. Our job is to make certain that we are centering our lives upon the truth. Knowing the Word of God is essential to developing discernment, making wise choices, and building our lives upon a solid foundation.

As Paul wrote, "I pray that the eyes of your heart may be enlightened, so that you will know what is the hope of His calling."[8]

---

[5] "G2583 - kanōn," *Strong's Greek Lexicon* (NIV), Blue Letter Bible, https://www.blueletterbible.org//lang/lexicon/lexicon.cfm?Strongs=g2583&t=niv.

[6] F. F. Bruce, *The Canon of Scripture* (Downers Grove: Intervarsity Press, 1988), 17–18.

[7] Jude 1:3.

[8] Ephesians 1:8 NASB.

ABOUT GOD'S WILL

God's will for our lives is much simpler than we make it out to be. In short, His will is that we receive salvation through Jesus' redemptive work at the cross, and then we become like Christ (sanctified). It is a one-time confession of sin and acceptance of Christ's sacrifice followed by a lifetime of yielding to His leading. A concise and demystifying definition of the will of God is this: "Be holy like Jesus, by the power of the Spirit, for the glory of God."[9] As we walk with God, our lives reflect Him. And the question remains: *how much control does God have and what freedom do we have?*

One perspective is God's complete sovereignty over all of life. Everything is destined to be as it is. With this perspective, we seek God for every choice and stress over decisions that may be insignificant. Or alternatively, if we're not seeking or stressing, we could be sitting back. If God is in control of every detail, we could coast through life, waiting for God to insert His will. In this, we could potentially waste much of our lives waiting. Pray over everything or do nothing. If this is how God's will is, then the human experience is incredibly difficult or terribly boring.

A different perspective of God's will involves our participation. A loving father lets his children make choices because love is a choice. He wants us to choose Him and engage in a life centered on knowing and serving Him. Love isn't love if you require the loved one to love you. He gave us free will to choose Him for salvation and to choose Him in our daily life.

As we go through life, we experience gifts bestowed upon us or troubles thrust upon us. A new job, a new home, a spouse, a child—these are gifts from God. Alternatively, hard things such as disease, death, and financial problems are allowed into our lives. We have little or no control over these things, nor do we even want these problems. But in His wisdom, the Lord allows

---

[9] Kevin DeYoung, *Just Do Something* (Chicago: Moody Publishers, 2009), 59.

them so we can become more like His Son. In the hardships, we can choose to honor God and build our relationship with Him. In this way, we work with Him and His will to create the lives we are living.

In *The Will of God as a Way of Life*, Jerry Sittser states, "God's sovereignty operates on two planes of reality. It does not contradict human freedom; rather, it envelops human freedom as a circle envelops a line drawn inside it."[10] God's sovereign control, order, and leadership—His metaview—wraps around our free will, preferences, and desires. What we can see is limited. The smaller story of our lives lies inside His expansive story of the history of the world.

VISION IS A QUALITY TO CULTIVATE

In business, mission and vision statements are created as foundational and inspirational declarations. These cornerstone pieces serve as a basis for decision-making and action planning. A mission statement declares the organization's core purpose; it states what the organization is, and what it is not. A vision statement is aspirational, telling the desired future result. It is inspiring and provides a clear picture of where the organization is headed. It motivates people to do the daily work because the overall goal is clear and meaningful.

Businesses lacking a mission and vision drift. Without the common knowledge of what the organization does and why it exists, setting strategy and making decisions are difficult. These statements provide grounding.

Our mission is simple. God's mission (His will) for our lives is in three parts: that we would know Him personally (salvation), then grow in Him (sanctification), and live with Him forever in heaven (glorification). That's it.

Vision is unique to each person. We are all given personalities, life experiences, talents, and opportunities. These personal

---

[10] Jerry Sittser, *The Will of God as a Way of Life* (Grand Rapids: Zondervan, 2004), 209.

pieces are meant for us to ponder, pick up, and put together for our journeys. We sense a pull or a notion and develop a vision. Then we must take it and apply the litmus test of Scripture. We can prayerfully consider the best timing, approach, and fit.

Leaders are often described as "visionary," and vision is a character quality we can develop. J. Oswald Sanders' classic book *Spiritual Leadership* says vision contains two delightful aspects—optimism and hope. "Vision leads to venture ... . The person of vision takes fresh steps of faith across gullies and chasms, not 'playing it safe' but neither taking foolish risks."[11]

It's vision that keeps us from aimless drifting. Vision is the sail that catches wind and takes us on our course across the water. Our only job is to make certain that our vision is godly and that we go after it.

QUESTIONS FOR REFLECTION

- In what ways do I see God's bigger picture wrapping around my narrow view ... my small contributions to His bigger plan?

- God's will for my life is that I know Him personally, then grow in Him, then live with Him eternally. How are my activities, goals, and desires in line with His will?

- Take stock of my personality traits, life experiences, talents, and opportunities. How do these things point toward a vision for my life?

---

[11] J. Oswald Sanders, *Spiritual Leadership* (Chicago: Moody Publishers, 1994), 57.

3

The Dirty Little Secret behind *The Secret*

And the Cure to Come Clean

When my oldest son turned six, he requested a magic show for his birthday party. The illusionist we chose featured levitation as part of his show, and my son was enthralled with the idea. Weeks later, an audience of kindergartners sat cross-legged on the floor while Steven played the role of magician's assistant. Before long, the illusionist had Steven lying on a board covered by a tablecloth and supported by two chairs. With the sleight of hand, he appeared to free-float. Wide-eyed kids ooo'd and aah'd. Later, my husband asked, "How did that feel?" Our new six-year-old scrunched his nose and said, "Like I was lying on a board." Steven brightened up and added, "I was floating on a board!" Ah, how easily young ones can be fooled.

The Secret was a movie and a series of books that revived an old belief called the Law of Attraction. This concept states that we get what we are thinking about. If we think about a new job, it materializes. If we concentrate on money, a check lands in the mailbox. When we think of certain people, they call or come knocking. Most everyone has had at least one experience like this. And when asked, most people confirm they believe in the Law of Attraction.

Many Christians liken the Law of Attraction to Scripture, recalling Bible verses that tell us as a man "thinks in his heart, so is he."[12] We also discuss the practice of reaping and sowing that Jesus preached.[13] These are legitimate Scriptures—they come from God's mouth for our benefit. But is it possible we are taking these Scriptures out of context and attaching them to concepts that were never meant to go together? Is it possible that we have too readily accepted a philosophy that appears to make sense but may not be beneficial in the end?

The Bible is not a self-help book. Taking verses here and there is like choosing only the items you like from the buffet and neglecting the full dining experience. We need the spinach salad, not only the decadent dessert. Choosing simply what we like leads to malnourishment, making us unhealthy in every way. We may like the Scriptures about abundant life and Jesus' miraculous healings, yet it is the acknowledgment of our sin-sick souls that makes the miracles more profound. We may reach for soothing psalms when we are weary, yet it is the context of David's peril that makes them more than poetry. Picking our favorites and leaving the rest is the way to errant theology. It leaves us open to the world's dangers and facades.

WHAT IS A VISION BOARD?

Years ago, we simply put posters, ticket stubs, and photos of friends and dream vacations on bulletin boards. My teenage bedroom was decked out with a cork wall, which I filled with my favorite things. A vision board is similar, but less random and more intentional. The process includes choosing images that signify what we want and what we see in our mind's eye.

---

[12] Proverbs 23:7 KJV.

[13] See also Galatians 6:7.

It is a fun and artistic activity. Some people post pictures on a poster board, some use a blank book, and some size it to fit inside a picture frame. The materials do not matter as much as the end product's application.

The vision board takes on a new level when we start talking about manifesting our desires. To "manifest" simply means that something is made clear or evident. When an idea or a goal or a project comes to fruition, it is manifested. We have sayings such as "What you think about, you bring about" and "Achieving starts with believing." There is a measure of truth to these adages—our involvement brings things to reality.

It bears considering who gets the praise for realized dreams. When desires manifest in life, should the individual receive congratulations on a job well done? Does the universe get credit? Where does God, the Giver of all good things, fit into the scenario? Having ideas, dreams, and visions is a common human experience (proof of a fully alive and thinking brain). Yet, many people take vision to mystical levels. The Law of Attraction provides a spiritualized response to manifesting dreams and visions.

THE LAW OF ATTRACTION

The Law of Attraction presumes everything in the universe is energy, positive or negative. LOA teachers state that the mind's thoughts are a form energy. Thoughts consist of light, sound, and heat, and they throw off particles into the atmosphere.[14] According to Massachusetts Institute of Technology (MIT), human thoughts are electrochemical reactions. The brain contains approximately a hundred billion nerve cells (or neurons) interconnected by trillions of connections (or synapses). When neurons connect with a new thought, such as when we read or learn, it is like an electrical connection.[15] But it does not become matter emitting into the universe.

---

[14] Neil E. Farber, *Throw Away Your Vision Board* (North Charleston: CreateSpace, 2014), 27–29.

[15] Elizabeth Dougherty, "What Are Thoughts Made Of?," *Ask an Engineer, MIT School of Engineering*, April 26, 2011.

As for "like attracting like," think about jumping a car battery. Both positive and negative energies are necessary. A battery attracts and repels. LOA advocates take this to mean that our thoughts possess the power to attract or repel things and circumstances. "The magnetic power of LOA apparently reaches out from your thoughts into the universe and attracts the things that are the same positive or negative vibrational level."[16] Under this system, every thought we have is responsible for everything in our lives. Whether things are going well or poorly, LOA teaches that we manifested it.

Proponents of LOA tie it to quantum physics, which is the science of particles (smaller than atoms) and their behavior. Scientists have discovered that particles behave both as matter and waves.[17] This is appealing to those who ascribe to metaphysics, the philosophy of the nature of reality and existence of God. But finding hard data or studies revealing a clear scientific link between LOA and quantum physics is nearly impossible. In fact, one academic journal states, "No qualified physicist would claim these kinds of connections [LOA and quantum physics] without committing fraud."[18]

Fully integrating LOA into life is a learned skill. The LOA cottage industry features seminars, books, and products on the subjects of vision boards, LOA, metaphysics, and techniques for successful use. Those who practice LOA in its purest sense rely on their positive thoughts to bring them the life and the things they desire. If "like attracts like," then planning and goal setting and deadline dates are construed as negative activity. These things effectively "cancel" the vision because action tells the universe we doubt its ability to come through for us.

---

[16] Daniel J. Maritz and Henk G. Stoker, "Does the Christian Worldview Provide a Place for the Law of Attraction?" (Part 1): An Apologetic Evalu-ation of the Roots of this Doctrine," *Verbum et Ecclesia* 37, no. 1 (July 27, 2016): 1–9.

17 Chad Orzel, "Six Things Everyone Should Know about Quantum Physics," *Forbes*, July 8, 2015, 6.

[18] Maritz and Stoker, 5.

Instead, simply believing or "stepping into" the vision is the correct behavior. It is also taught that associating with negative people creates bad energy. Things like support groups or serving at a soup kitchen may not help manifest one's vision.[19] With all these rules and techniques running counter to mainstream thinking, it is no wonder followers attend multiple (expensive) seminars.

On the contrary, living our best life is not a matter of sending our wishes out to a faceless force known as the universe. We can talk to the Creator of the universe, who wants to give us something greater than our hollow wishes.

THERE IS NOTHING NEW UNDER THE SUN

One of the first words a toddler typically learns is "mine." Little ones want their toys, their food, their way. Practically from birth, we think we know what is best for us. We have a fierce and driving need to be the director of our lives and the master of our agendas.

After my crisis of faith when I wondered about my bold business prayers, I returned to the traditional and methodical thinking of my upbringing. I posted charts to track sales and progress toward company incentives. I posted pictures of the trips and incentives I worked toward, the sofa I wished for, and pictures of happy-looking women working at home. I tracked results, made lists, and carefully planned my steps. Yes, I prayed over these things, but in retrospect I held tightly to my desires and my actions.

We possess a deep desire for control and to call the shots in our own lives. While God gave us the gift of choice, we often choose to go it alone when we simply don't have to. In her book *The Longing in Me*, Sheila Walsh explains the rub we feel when it comes to personal control. "There's only one cure for this devastating sickness of the soul. It's a radical surrender

---

[19] Neil Farber, "The Truth about the Law of Attraction—It Doesn't Exist," *Psychology Today*, September 18, 2016, https://www.psychologytoday.com/blog/the-blame-game/201609/the-truth-about-the-law-attraction.

of everything you are and have, everything you love and hold dear, to the sovereign control of God. That's not easy to do or even tempting, unless you are utterly convinced that God is good and He is for you."[20] Yes, He is good and He is for us. Can we release our strongholds and fall into His safety net?

Ever since the garden, we've been a people craving knowledge, power, and independence. We let enticements tickle our fancy. The Genesis account reveals the slippery slope of sin. What the serpent did to Eve millennia ago, the world does to us today. We are led to doubt God's authority and promises—His goodness—and help ourselves to heaping spoonfuls of selfishness.

God set eternity and a desire for forward momentum in our hearts. Yet we tend to desire lush living over living for the Lamb. We tend to take matters into our own hands and not trust the hand of God. Purpose, passion, and even pretty little things all come from His good hand. Yes, God is good and He is for us.

HOW THE LAW OF ATTRACTION BEGAN

Indeed, there is nothing new under the sun. The origins of the Law of Attraction date back to Greco-Roman mythology, in which Hermes was a messenger god, going back and forth between this world and the spirit world. He was the guide for the living and brought luck. The fact that this god was also the spirit accompanying souls to the afterlife made him especially mystical and esoteric. Followers of Hermes left many writings, and perhaps the most well-known is the Emerald Tablet. Considered a "code," it contained details of the scientific philosophy of alchemy, or the "treasures of science."[21]

---

[20] Sheila Walsh, *The Longing in Me* (Nashville: Nelson Books, 2016), 60, Kindle.
[21] Florian Ebeling, Jan Assmann, and David Lorton, *The Secret History of Hermes Trismegistus: Hermeticism from Ancient to Modern Times*, 1st ed. (Ithaca: Cornell University Press, 2007), 46–48.

Paul warned against this very thing when he wrote to the church in Colossae. Mythology was alive and well, and the church struggled with heresy as followers blended Greek philosophy and mysticism with the gospel. "See to it that no one takes you captive through hollow and deceptive philosophy, which depends on human tradition and the elemental spiritual forces of this world rather than on Christ."[22] What Paul said to the Colossians is true for us—be on guard; it is far too easy to fall into worldly thinking!

Fast-forward to the nineteenth century as science leaped and bounded its way from a common knowledge of God as Creator. In the United States, Charles Darwin was making his case for evolution, the railroad was connecting the country from east to west, and all forms of transportation and automation were making life faster and easier. This growing independence from God resulted in a shift toward deism, the belief in one impersonal and uninvolved God. Science penetrated the culture with the message that matter (aka atoms) exists eternally, but God does not exist.[23] In short, a rejection of God spread. This fertile foundation allowed the New Thought movement to take root.

THE NEW THOUGHT MOVEMENT

The father of New Thought and clockmaker by day, Phineas Quimby dabbled in hypnosis on the side. He eventually developed the idea of mind healing. He believed the mind shaped one's reality, and illness was the result of negative thinking.

Ralph Waldo Trine, the next major influential thinker of this movement, took the concept of mind healing to another level to include personal achievement. Trine rejected the ultimate authority of Scripture, stating other religions' writings were also holy and beneficial. He rejected salvation through Christ and instead taught unity with the Infinite. He stated that people limit themselves when they limit their point of

---

[22] Colossians 2:8.

[23] James Sire, *The Universe Next Door*, 5th ed. (Downers Grove: InterVarsity Press, 2009), 67–68.

view to one religion.[24] Millions bought his best-selling books, which were rich with Christian verbiage, unaware they were reading material contrary to biblical precepts.

New Thought teachers rapidly emerged and made numerous and lasting changes upon culture. From this movement the Christian Science, Unity, and Unitarian Universalist churches began. The self-help movement exploded with books and seminars. There are literally thousands of New Thought teachers, preachers, and authors today.

The New Thought philosophy focuses on health and wealth through positive thoughts, metaphysics, and spirituality. Core beliefs include humans as in control of our destiny and powerful over our lives, independent from God or the need of a Savior. Jesus Christ is seen as a moral teacher and salvation is seen as mystical oneness with the universe. Depravity of sin has given way to ethical behavior. Beliefs such as these are attractive because sin is not something we like to address and submission to God is even less desirable. We are naturally prone to seek systems to follow and works to perform to appease God and maintain control over our lives.

New Thought philosophy has penetrated nearly every aspect of our modern culture. Not surprisingly, the church has also been affected.

THE WORD OF FAITH MOVEMENT

A pastor and evangelist during the late eighteen hundreds and early nineteen hundreds, E. W. Kenyon presented a brand of theology that included "positive confession." He coined statements such as, "What I confess, I possess."[25] Kenyon did not ascribe to the belief of Jesus' sacrifice on the cross. He stated that the cross had no power; it was a place of failure where Christ suffered and died. This view sorely overlooks and

---

[24] David W. Jones and Russell S. Woodbridge, *Health, Wealth & Happiness: Has the Prosperity Gospel Overshadowed the Gospel of Christ?* (Grand Rapids: Kregel Publications, 2011), 27–33.

[25] Ibid., 51–52.

discredits the sacrifice Christ made on our behalf and the pain of bearing our sins. It also dismisses His miraculous ascension.

Word of Faith is not any one church but a classification of an errant strain of theology. The name derived from the movement's emphasis on the power of words. Advocates teach a kind of faith in having faith and speaking faith-filled words. Faith becomes a matter of focus and force in prayer, positive confession, and speaking scriptural phrases, as if to manipulate God to do what one desires.[26]

Word of Faith teaching sounds much like the American dream—a home, a nice car or two in the garage, vacations, peace, health, happiness, and apple pie. It is not a far-fetched to say most television preachers come from this heretical ideology. TV sermons tend to talk of the benefits of following God, and this appeals to us. Years ago, Kenyon said, "The value in Christianity is what we get out of it."[27] In contrast, the gospel message talks of sacrifice, a life of service, and even persecution. It is not hard to determine the message the masses prefer to follow.

Word of Faith teaching has several features that are not consistent with Scripture. First, people are the central figures in their lives, rather than centering their lives on God. Word of Faith teachers elevate humans to godlike status with statements such as, "You don't have a God in you, you are one."[28] Second, they reject the Trinity. Father, Son, and Holy Spirit are not three in one, coequal and coeternal. Instead, God manifests Himself as one or the other for different purposes. Third, they minimize Christ as a member of the Trinity, and belief is mainly for purposes of living one's ideal life; therefore, His work at the cross is no longer crucial. While salvation is taught, sin is often left out.

---

[26] Maritz and Stoker, 6.

[27] Quoted in Jones and Woodbridge, 52–53.

[28] Hank Hanegraaff, *Christianity in Crisis: 21st Century* (Nashville: Thomas Nelson, 2009), 134.

But if redemption from sin is not a requirement of salvation, then what are we saved from and what are we saved for? Mind-over-matter faith minimizes salvation as a mere component of successful living. Beware, because God cannot be mocked.[29] Offering the Creator of the universe and the lover of our souls a flippant faith and a pious list of accomplishments is a charade.

Word of Faith is not much different from New Thought or Law of Attraction or mythology. In short, all these beliefs put the self in the center of one's life, for the pleasures of life. The only difference with the Word of Faith is that it is wrapped in Scripture. The real treasure of our life in Christ is cast aside for a cheap imitation.

LEARNING TO DISCERN

Since the garden, we've been following things that promise much but return little. It is the enemy who twists God's truths into dangerous deceptions. History, literature, and science shape each generation's culture, influencing the way we see and experience our world. With each generation, the enemy lurks, ready to mix his deviant cocktail du jour.

And we drink.

He does it again and again, decade after decade, duping the undiscerning.

Perhaps, dear one, you've been hurt by mind-over-matter thinking, the Law of Attraction, or the Word of Faith. It's everywhere in our culture and in our churches. It pops up when we least expect it.

The solution is to know God's Word; to sniff out the lie and turn the other way. True success does not come from following five easy steps to a sweet life. True success is obedience to God's Word.

Let's not fall for the illusion like those kindergartners at the magic show birthday party. "Let us stop going over the basic

---

[29] Galatians 6:7–8.

teachings about Christ again and again. Let us go on instead and become mature in our understanding."[30] Let's grow up in our faith, understanding the entirety of the Word, not bits and pieces of Scripture.

We must learn to discern.

❧

Many years ago, my husband was fighting a battle with an incurable cancer. Just a week after receiving the bad news, a mom from our kids' Christian school stopped me in the parking lot. I had just dropped off my children, an ordinary routine, shrouded by the shock and sadness of our circumstances.

In her attempt to offer comfort, this well-meaning woman brought pain and confusion. Steve's diagnosis was not of God, she said. All good and perfect gifts are from God, she said. She went on. The enemy comes to steal, kill, and destroy. Disease is of the enemy, and God would heal him if we would only pray boldly and believe.

I couldn't believe what I was hearing. My sick husband was fighting cancer, not a spiritual battle because of a lack of faith. I thanked her for her concern. I shared that we were embarking on a trial from which we would learn and grow closer to God and to each other. I shared our belief that our lives were in God's hands and each day is a gift.

And then I excused myself, got in my car, and cried.

In short, Word of Faith heresy hurts people.

Word of Faith puts unbiblical expectations on us to fix what is wrong, and if we are not healthy and wealthy, we are probably under Satan's thumb. If we are sick, our lack of faith caused it. If we are not healed, our lack of believing prayer is to blame. If bad things happen, we were not claiming the goodness of God over our lives.

What damage this causes our souls!

---

[30] Hebrews 6:1 NLT.

UNPACK THE BAGGAGE

Matthew recounts Jesus' reply to an inquiring wealthy man: "Sell all your possessions and give to the poor." The disciples were astonished. Jesus continued, "It is easier for a camel to go through the eye of a needle than for a rich man to enter the kingdom of God."[31] He used this exaggeration to make a point.

Kingdoms and cities were once walled. City gates provided the only way in and out for visitors, deliveries, or travelers of any sort. In Jerusalem, the main gates closed at night, and the side gate was used after sundown. This side gate, which still stands today, is known as The Eye of the Needle Gate because it is small and narrow. Camels were unloaded of riders and baggage, then stooped to pass through. For entrance into the kingdom of heaven, we must reverently unloose ourselves of everything that hinders our faith.

We must bow down and surrender everything that weighs us down and holds us back, including incorrect and unhelpful attitudes and beliefs, errant teaching, worldly influences, dangerous and defiant practices. And sin. We cannot forget that, either.

Get off that treadmill that leads nowhere. "It is for freedom that Christ has set us free."[32] Loose yourself from the yolk of slavery. You are free from the work of fixing your life yourself; you never could in the first place. Let your Redeemer do it for you and guide you to a fresh, free faith in Him.

If you have been following any of these beliefs or thought patterns, confess it now. Unpack what is not scriptural and leave it at the gate.

As the father of the epileptic son cried, "Lord, I believe; help my unbelief!"[33] Only through wholehearted devotion to God and knowing Him through His Word can we believe as Jesus taught.

---

[31] 19:16–26.

[32] Galatians 5:1.

[33] Mark 9:24 NKJV.

QUESTIONS FOR REFLECTION

- Are there any ways my faith reflects a "faith in faith"? On the other hand, how does my faith reflect faith in the one true God?

- How might my prayers attempt to will God to do as I wish? How can I adopt an attitude of a surrendered heart?

- What are my personal areas of unbelief?

4

Wired for Vision and Victory

Laura was a single mom of four young children who bravely believed life could get better. She got the idea to create a vision book with images and ideas signifying what she wanted her new life to look like. Flipping through magazines and tearing out inspiring images became a purposeful activity. She eventually involved her kids, encouraging them to think of the family they were reconstructing. They began to dream again and have fun; vision boarding proved to be therapeutic. Laura discovered many things she wanted, including a peaceful home and a loving second marriage.

God used the life-altering event of divorce to woo her to Himself. After years of misunderstanding Christianity, her heart began softening. When she met David, he was a new believer. His exuberant new faith mixed with their blooming love opened the way for Laura to understand salvation. She received Christ, and a diamond ring followed not long after. Years later, she still looks at her vision book and adds to it. Recently she noticed the picture of a married couple she glued in her book long ago. The man in the photo looked just like … David!

How can this be?

How did this vision grow from a wish in her heart to the man in her arms? How did Cami, Katie, and Kathleen show up to become representatives on my sales team? For that matter, how does any hope or dream materialize? If it's not metaphysics, what then?

EVERYTHING WE NEED

The last few summers, I have taken on a new hobby, growing a small vegetable garden. Most every summer morning, I step outside to check the flower beds and vegetable garden. I water when needed, adjust soil and add nutrients, and get a little excited when something is ripe and ready to be picked. No houseplant of mine has made it more than a few months. But growing something outside in summertime has been a remarkably easy, pleasing hobby.

Gardeners describe the process of caring for perennials in three steps. First, the newly planted bulbs "sleep" the first season they are transplanted. The second year, the plant grows a little more; it "creeps." The third season, the plant takes off in size and blooms; it "leaps."

We, too, have a natural desire to grow. Second Corinthians 5:9 says that we aspire to please Him. What a goal—to please God. We can sow seeds, deepen our roots of confident faith, and cultivate a life that bears fruit. We have everything we need to do this; we only need to remain close to God and work with His design.

We are dearly loved by the Creator and made in His triune image. He is Father, Son, and Holy Spirit. Humans also exist in three parts: body, soul, and spirit. While God exists three persons in one, we exist three parts in struggle. Yet there is hope! God has given us everything we need for living a godly life.[34] We receive all we need by coming to know Him. If there is any secret to life, that would be it—to know God.

---

[34] 2 Peter 1:3 NLT.

We are made body, soul, and spirit. The body is also known as the flesh. It is the material substance of a person, and it includes the brain. The soul consists of one's emotions, will, and intellect. The spirit is the secret inner core and true essence of a person; it is the spirit that communes with God. The spirit acts upon the soul, and the soul expresses itself through the body. The soul is the interchange between body and spirit. One's entire being is directed by the soul, the source of will and volition.[35]

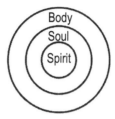

Before we are saved by faith in Jesus Christ, the body, soul, and spirit are unregenerate and resistant to God. Upon salvation, we are awakened.[36] The Holy Spirit takes up residence in us to quicken our spirits and commune with us. Thanks to the Holy Spirit, we go from a state of languish to the supernatural ability to flourish. He has given us everything we need for living a godly life!

GUARD THE HEART

The heart is the soul. All day long, the soul is barraged with thoughts and emotions to process, followed by choices to make. Obey the flesh and sin or obey the spirit and have peace. It is no wonder Scripture repeatedly advises, "Guard your heart." Guard the heart, for everything you do flows from it.[37]

---

[35] Watchman Nee, *The Spiritual Man* (New York: Christian Fellowship Publishers, Inc., 1968), 31.

[36] Priscilla Shirer, *Discerning the Voice of God* (Chicago: Moody Publishers, 2007), 29.

[37] Proverbs 4:23.

Cognitive psychology is the study of how humans process information. An extremely shortened example follows. First, we receive information (stimulus), then we process thoughts and emotions, and this is followed by a response on our part.

If we don't guard our hearts, we can process a friend's warm greeting with contempt. "I can't stand cheerful morning people! I wish she would leave me alone to drink my coffee in peace and quiet!" From these negative thoughts may come grumbling, complaining, and a poor way to start the day. Not to mention, the tearing down of a friendship.

The primary function of the brain is to protect and keep us alive. This includes urgent safety, such as removing fingers from a hot stove or the need to slow down and sleep away a fever. The brain's function of keeping us safe also extends to keeping our thoughts harmonious. When our attitudes, beliefs, and behavior are inconsistent, they weigh us down, nag at us, and make us generally unhappy. This is known as cognitive dissonance.

Counselors, therapists, and life coaches offer strategies to clear the dissonance. When we reach a state of uncertainty, confusion, or disharmony, it is a red flag. This is the time to remember that the soul often battles between body and spirit. Reaching for the Word or stopping to pray is a good response. Without aligning our thoughts to the Lord, we are left to our own devices of justifying, evading, or forging ahead with what feels good.

Seek the Lord's guidance and choose better. This function of the brain is a built-in "check and balance" gift of God.

MAKING OUR VISIONS A REALITY

Creating a collage or a vision board and viewing it regularly bring you joy. Studies show that viewing art motivates the brain's neural systems. Art is pleasurable, and when we view art, the body's dopamine levels increase.[38] This is one reason why vision boards are popular—because they simply make people happy.

The production of "happy chemicals" encourages us toward achieving goals.[39] Dopamine produces feelings of joy. Oxytocin produces feelings of safety and bonding with others. Serotonin produces feelings of respect and pride. Endorphins bring on feelings of euphoria and mask pain. These are all beneficial when we venture out, try something new, and endeavor to achieve great things.

In addition to simply feeling happy, the actual process of creating a vision board helps us sort out and clarify our thoughts. Cognitive dissonance gives way to consonance, or clarity of thought. When we feel clarity, another dose of hormones courses through the body and we feel good.

When we begin to focus on our vision, goals, and desires, the interesting phenomenon of cognitive bias pops up. Since the brain's job is to keep us safe, it is constantly seeking information to match the outer world with our inner world. Aligning thoughts, emotions, and beliefs is part of the brain's one-track mind of safety. Cognitive bias explains why we tend to easily find others in the same boat as we are. For instance, when traveling in a foreign country, we tend to find others from our culture speaking our language. The brain is cleverly looking out for us.

Cognitive bias is part of the reason why vision boards "work." We mount pictures of our heart's desire, which engages the brain to seek these things out for us. When we step out in faith to do something new, cognitive bias is the reason it seems the world rises up to meet us.

This starts an upward cycle of positivity. When we take small steps toward our goal, happy chemicals are released. We

---

[38] Dahlia W. Zaidel, "Art and Brain: Insights from Neuropsychology, Biology and Evolution," *Journal of Anatomy* (2010): 216

[39] Loretta Graziano Breuning, *Habits of a Happy Brain* (Avon, MA: Adams Media Publishing, 2016), 14.

are encouraged and continue onward. When we break large tasks into smaller ones and make progress, those positive hormones fire. Celebrating small victories triggers more dopamine, as well as endorphins that make us feel invincible.[40] Our dreams are coming true and we are on top of the world.

When we are fully engaged, living out our vision and accomplishing great things, we are in full-on creative mode. Everyone has the capacity to be creative. In its simplest and most universal definition, creativity is the "ability to produce work that is novel and useful" or original and adaptive.[41] Positive emotions of love, joy, and curiosity are linked to creativity. This then produces positive hormones, and the upward cycle of good things continues.

MENTAL PREPARATION, A POWERFUL ACHIEVEMENT TOOL

After Shaun White's 2018 Olympic gold medal snowboard run, he told a sports reporter that he repeatedly visualized his routine. The practice of mental rehearsal, imagery, and visualization is key in the field of sports psychology. The concept springs from what is known about the brain creating memories from repetition. After neuropathways have been created, it's as if the brain has worn a groove. It becomes natural to perform the winning routine, for example.

Imagery simulates a true sensory experience. One must see the scenario, feel, smell, hear, and taste the experience. Real and imagined stimuli produce similar effects on the conscious.[42] We can visualize one-time events, such as an athletic competition, and also repeat positive thoughts of achieving great things. This hardwires the brain to experience successful results in all of life.

---

[40] Breuning, 144.

[41] Wendy Suzuki, *Healthy Brain, Happy Life* (New York: Harper Collins, 2015), 217.

[42] Michael Bar-Eli, *Boost* (New York: Oxford University Press, 2018), 226–227.

ℭℐ

A leader in a direct sales company, Lisa used the power of visualization to rise to the top. Several years ago, she sat in the audience at her company's national conference and watched many representatives receive recognition for sales excellence. She realized that to be in that elite category, she was short by just $1,000 in sales. Enthusiasm mingled with prayer. She felt in her spirit she should do this.

Over the next six months, she ran a movie through her mind of walking across the stage and receiving her award. To reach this sales goal, she had to surpass her previous personal best. Her commitment to do the work and achieve the goal outweighed any misgivings, fears, or limitations. Every night she tracked her progress and every morning she visualized her success. Day by day and sale by sale, she visualized her way to achievement.

Not surprisingly, she earned the distinctive award. It also came with a nice bonus check, which she donated to mission work. For Lisa, it wasn't about the money. It was about expanding her potential. Since then, she has earned many more awards and trips. Travelling the world enlarged her comfort zone beyond her small town, a personal benefit she could not have foreseen. Visualizing a stretch goal many years ago resulted in a true personal and professional turning point.

WE LIVE BY FAITH

Abraham's life included moral failures and sins, as well as repentance, humility, and transformation. He had taught his soul to obey the Lord more fully and more often than not. When Abraham was well past one hundred years of age, God put him to the test. He was to journey to Mount Moriah and sacrifice his beloved son, Isaac.

Genesis 22 explains that the morning after receiving God's commandment, Abraham chopped wood for the sacrifice. Sharing none of the details with Sarah and Isaac, he loaded up his donkey, gathered two servants and Isaac, and they set out for the three-day journey. On the third day with the hill in sight, Abraham said to his servants, "Stay here with the donkey while I and the boy go over there. We will worship and then we will come back to you."[43]

Upon reaching the hilltop, Isaac asked, "Where is the lamb for the burnt offering?" Amazingly, Isaac's faith mirrors his father's. As a teenage boy, he could have overpowered his elderly father. Instead, he willingly let his father wrap him up and place him on the altar. Perhaps their hearts were pounding or perhaps they had a supernatural calm, but just as Abraham raised a knife over his beloved son, an angel appeared.

"Abraham! Abraham! Do not lay a hand on the boy. Do not do anything to him. Now I know that you fear God, because you have not withheld from me your son, your only son."[44] As Abraham acknowledged the angel, he noticed a ram stuck in the bushes. It was the ram that was sacrificed that day, and Abraham named the hilltop The Lord Will Provide.

After a lifetime of following God and listening to His commands, Abraham knew God's ways. His response to this ultimate test is remarkable. We, too, can have a faith like this. Following the Lord day in and day out produces character when we are put to the test. Abraham's telltale signs of mature character are:

Obedience. Abraham did not deliberate God's command. He did not beg and plead for his son's life, nor did he avoid God. Furthermore, he acted immediately. The following morning, he prepared and followed through. There was no grabbing the calendar to see when he could fit God in.

Compassion. Abraham did not mention any details of the sacrifice to Sarah or to Isaac. Imagine the trouble he could have created and the difficulty in following God if he had opened his mouth. Not to mention, excessive or negative chatter may have eroded the sense of holiness of this event. Abraham showed

---

[43] v. 5.
[44] Genesis 22:11–12.

love for his family and leadership over his household by communing only with God.

Confidence. Abraham told his two servants to wait with the donkey while he and Isaac ascended the hill to worship, and said "we" will return. Abraham knew God would intervene somehow. Whether it meant a ram appearing in a bush or resurrecting his sacrificed son, Abraham had complete confidence in God. He did not forget God's promise of long ago, that many nations would be his legacy, and therefore, Isaac could not be killed. Abraham trusted and surrendered, fully confident in God.

Developing these character traits takes time, as we see in Abraham's life and experience in our own lives. The pathway to strengthening these traits is willingness. If we are willing to respect and listen, we can develop obedience. If we are willing to care, we can become more compassionate. If we are willing to trust God's Word, it will lead to confidence. And if we are willing to let go of our own will (our willful stubbornness), we can accept God's will.

⁊

The Lord is asking us today, *What do you love most?*

He beckons us to surrender our hopes and dreams and our greatest loves, to let go of our ideas, our self-willed plans, our carefully construed calendars.

When we release these things from our clutches and place them in God's good hand, we are free. Instead of emptiness when we give it all to God, we find the fullness of His grace and the capacity to truly love.

Plant the seeds of character and grow a life of aspiring to please God. Total obedience. Sweet compassion. Complete confidence. Unbridled faith. This is the way to visionary, victorious living.

QUESTIONS FOR REFLECTION

- If my life is led by my soul (emotions, will, and intellect), how can I care for my soul?

- What thoughts and behaviors need reassessing to align more closely to Scripture and the heart of God?

- Abraham demonstrated obedience, compassion, and confidence. How do I possess these qualities and how can I grow in these areas?

5

The Paradoxes of Promise

A Biblical Framework for Life-Building

Hello, my name is Julie, and I am an HGTV addict. I admit it—that channel is the default when I turn on the tube. I am not crafty; I am a hot mess with a hot glue gun. I do not dare to refinish dressers or reupholster chairs. But massive remodeling projects, that's my game. I don't do the work, but I can manage the project like a boss. We're talking total overhaul of both homes I've owned. As a business geek and a home remodeler, it's no surprise my favorite TV shows are house-flipping shows.

These shows center on investors working on a deadline to gut the home, fix it up, and sell it hopefully for a tidy profit. Things get interesting once demolition begins. Any number of problems from faulty wiring, bad plumbing, or mold are often found. The most detrimental issue is a bad foundation. In worst-case situations, floors, walls, and doors are not level. This threatens the entire structure, making the home unsafe.

A beautiful home constructed on a bad foundation lacks its full value because it is uninhabitable. The good news is, it can be fixed. There are tools, experts, and methods to restore the integrity of the home and fulfill its potential as a home of beauty and function.

The foundation of a Christian's life is Christ, the solid rock. A life built upon personal redemption found only at the cross provides the solid foundation. From there, the lifelong work of sanctification begins. Sanctification simply means the process of growing into the image of Christ. A redeemed and sanctified life is made beautiful because of Christ's love and useful for the sharing of His love. Ultimately, this is the will of God for you.

How we work out the exact details of His will in our lives is unique to each one of us. He made us with unique personalities and a specific set of gifts, then placed us in this moment of history with the family and life experiences that are ours alone. Our uniqueness, along with the Word of God, provides the blueprint to build our one and only life.

❧

When I was a little girl, my dad and my grandpa spent many Saturdays remodeling our basement. My mother told me to leave them alone while they worked because there were sharp tools, long pieces of lumber and drywall, and lots of sawdust. A curious kid, I would tiptoe down the stairs, crack open the basement door, and peek.

One Saturday, my grandpa noticed me spying. He was the world's best grandpa because whenever he saw me, he smiled and his eyes twinkled. He didn't shoo me away; instead he welcomed me into their workroom.

From my five-year-old perspective, I'd thought it would take a few hours to make our basement into a fantastical playroom. My dad explained they were framing the walls and proceeded to show me their tools. The table saw looked scary, but the level was interesting. My dad crouched down behind me, put the level against the wall, and tipped it a little to the left, a little to the right, and then perfectly horizontal. I saw that bubble slide around then settle in the center when Dad had it just right. There was a tool to let you know when something was straight. A fascinating tool for everything to fit in the end!

What if we could build our lives in Christ with a leveling tool? What we've learned so far is the simplicity of God's will for our lives, that is, to know Christ as Savior and grow in Him. We've also learned there is no one way to do this because we are all unique expressions of God. Still, what if we could put our visions, hopes, and dreams to the test? How can we determine if the things we wanted, God also wanted for us? When the pieces of our lives are straight as tested with a level, the design fits. Indeed, centuries ago the Bible was known as the Canon, literally meaning rod or rule.[45] Early Christians referred to God's Word as "rule of faith" as if saying the Word was their leveling tool.

Tools are simply aids for us to apply. There are two important things we must always remember. First, we are not tools. We are not robotic hands and feet the Lord plugs into place to do His bidding. He loves us and allows us to work with Him so that we can experience our faith. Second, the Christian life itself is not a tool. Our faith is not a formula or a series of if-then statements. God desires relationship with us, and He wants to do something good in us.

As demonstrated in Abraham, surrender allows our vision to take root. When we are willing to respect, willing to care, and willing to trust, we submit ourselves to the growth process. Our act of submission plants the small seeds of obedience to the Lord, compassion for people and pressing issues, and confidence in God's promise. From there, our character grows and our vision refines and aligns to God's best for us. We need a place to start. Reverential acknowledgment of who we are in relation to who God is—surrender—is like starting from the ground up.

---

[45] "G2583 - kanōn," *Strong's*.

BUSINESS STRATEGY AND REAL LIFE

Once an organization determines its mission and vision, then a solid plan can be developed. Strategy is what moves a business toward fulfilling its mission. There are many ways to perform a thorough business assessment and create strategy. Most assessments include the common elements of identifying the business's strengths and the potential opportunities. From there, objectives, goals, and action items can be set. The beauty of this process is the connectedness it yields. From business mission through to the current day's actions, everything ties together and leads toward the business's aspirations.

When a business chooses and sets goals, it must consider the resources needed to achieve the goals. Goals are supported by many things, such as human resource talent, knowledge, funding, technology, and more. Wise leaders do not charge full steam ahead without assessing resource needs. Too many resource gaps may mean the goal should be abandoned. The point is to maximize results and minimize risk.

In our personal lives, we also have an innate desire to maximize the return on our investment, so to speak. We are wired to desire maximum happiness and satisfaction for a low- or no-risk investment of our resources. When considering our vision, goals, and daily actions, there are four resource areas that make or break our plans: knowledge, competence, emotional and spiritual strength, and finances and other resources. If we are weak in these areas or lack them altogether (or perceive a lack), abandoning our vision and goals seems reasonable.

Or is it?

Do we, too, often rely on our human judgment, not allowing God to move in supernatural ways?

In 2011, I considered these things as I contemplated a new business. After more than a decade in direct sales, I wanted to return in some fashion to my former career in training and development. A segue into coaching and training leaders in direct sales seemed like a good use of my experience and strengths. I proceeded to fill a notebook with ideas and took months to pray about the switch. It seemed everything I did to that point had led me to this new business. My heart sang a resounding "yes" every time I prayed about it.

Knowing there was no way I could launch a business without my husband's support, I created a complete business plan. Just like contestants on *Shark Tank*, I gave a presentation for Steve. Thankfully, he was a kind "shark"! He understood the scope and potential and gave his full support. I enrolled in coaching school, set up my business, and slowly picked up clients. I soon included marketing via the internet and began conducting webinars. A business was born! Emotions swung from exhilaration on a good day to doubt on a bad day, but I pressed on.

Once I began, I realized how much I didn't know. Drawing clients to the business through internet marketing was my weakest link. Yet God provided for that gap of knowledge. I met wonderful people who offered pro bono help many times. I found a community of like-minded professionals through the internet and built a circle of support.

PARADOXES OF PROMISE

Clients come to me as a business coach to get clarity, then get into action. I ask questions based upon their unique business and circumstances and the client can draw the best answers from within.

Questions geared toward evaluation and reflection result in higher-level thinking and lead to sound judgments and decisions. When it comes to choosing what direction to go or dream to go after, a series of deeper questions is required.

Questions rooted in Scripture and designed to cause reflection will produce sound decisions. A paradox causes deeper-level thinking. One definition of the word *paradox* is

45

"a statement or proposition that seems self-contradictory or absurd but in reality, expresses a possible truth."[46] A paradox causes us to look beneath the surface and find nuggets of gold.

The Christian life is a paradox. Our lives are hidden in Christ.[47] In losing our life for Christ's sake, we find it.[48] We are free from sin and a slave to righteousness.[49] Our lives have great worth and life is but a vapor.[50] On the surface, these statements seem contradictory, even absurd, yet these are truths. A life in Christ is the treasure we seek, for Christ Himself is the treasure.[51]

Just like a leveling tool measures alignment in construction, the paradox is a tool to align our thoughts to Scripture. God gave us free will to make all our choices in life. As believers in Christ, we desire to live according to His will.

In our humanness, we go from dreaming to scheming in a heartbeat. Too often we are tempted to "DIY" our projects. Another common approach is to put off our plans due to analysis paralysis. Either way, we've forgotten God!

So how do we make the best choices and build lives that honor God?

Visioneering, a term coined by Andy Stanley, is an inside-out activity because vision comes from both the eyes of the heart and the mind's eye. Stanley says visionary people allow "their hearts and minds to wander outside the artificial boundaries imposed by the world as it is."[52]

Got an idea?

Great! Set the goal, select a target date, then figure out all the steps.

---

[46] "Paradox," Dictionary.com, http://www.dictionary.com/browse/paradox?s=t.

[47] Colossians 3:3.

[48] Matthew 10:39.

[49] Romans 6:18.

[50] James 4:14.

[51] Colossians 2:3.

[52] Stanley, *Visioneering*, 18.

"For the eyes of the Lord move to and fro throughout the earth that He may strongly support those whose heart is completely His."[53]

Did you catch that?

He wants to *strongly support* us!

We must depend on God instead of ourselves. He's in the business of the details and will answer the question we naturally ask: "How will these plans be accomplished?"

Be prepared because He will bring visions into reality in the most surprising ways. As we seek to align our hearts to His, we can have assurance that he has many promises in store for us. These paradoxes of promise test our dreams, visions, and plans and align them to Scripture. They provide a scale to consider as we build our lives. We can ask in prayer if we are growing closer toward or moving further from the Lord. We can meditate on the question of where our trust and dependence lie.

Do we trust in our knowledge, our abilities, our strength, our resources ... or the Lord's?

Our intelligence is found in His ultimate wisdom. When we are faithful to act upon and share what we know, God can use it for much greater purposes. It's not a test of our expertise; we simply need to be faithful stewards of the truth and knowledge we gather.

Our inadequacies are perfected in His sufficiency. Rather than feeling shame or worrying about our perceived inadequacy, choose humility. Rather than making endless efforts to be fully prepared, humbly tap the ultimate source of God's transformational love. Humility enables us to reach for help and accept its gifts.

Our weakness is His strength. The conduit between weakness and strength is courage. From a decision of the heart, courage is born and strengthened. Courage is the way to look challenge in the eye with little fear or discouragement.

Our lack is His abundance. The God who holds all time, space, and humanity in His hands lacks for nothing. Every

---

[53] 2 Chronicles 16:9 NASB.

resource under heaven is His. Hope is the key to unlock our limited view and see that anything is possible.

Inside these paradoxes are scriptural truths. We can assess our vision through the lens of Scripture. We can develop greater faithfulness, humility, courage, and hope. Vision becomes a way of life and a continuing project of life-building.

Like the level used in construction, these paradoxes align our lives and make straight our dreams, visions, and plans. No more DIY when we have the architect, the engineer, and the general manager on the job. "Unless the LORD builds the house, those who build it labor in vain."[54]

What could our lives look like if everything we are living for is of God?

Imagine a world full of exuberant, certain, confident, compassionate, peaceful, patient, loving, gracious, hopeful, joyful sons and daughters serving the King.

What a vision!

QUESTIONS FOR REFLECTION

- How have I functioned as the architect of my plans?

- What may come of my vision if I allow the Lord to strongly support me?

- How can I develop greater faithfulness, humility, courage, and hope? How might this help my vision?

- For my vision to come to fruition, it needs to be supported by knowledge, competence, strength, and finances and other resources. Assess these things and identify what is needed, what are the gaps, and how might the Lord strongly support me in these areas.

---

[54] Psalm 127:1 ESV.

6

Our Limited Knowledge inside God's Ultimate Wisdom

Esther 1–2

When Abraham gazed at the stars in the night sky, he could never have known that some fifteen hundred years later one of his descendants would be a star. Unlike the account of Abraham, who had the benefit of interaction with God, the story of Esther, Queen of Persia, leaves God out. Interestingly, the Lord is a silent party in this book of the Bible, remaining in the background, shaping and guiding events. A young woman immersed in Scripture, when her moment arrived, Esther had the strength to accomplish a great task. She was the original Wonder Woman because she bravely saved the Israelites from annihilation. No wonder her name means "star" in Persian.

Like Esther, we can prepare for our moment and watch for the Lord's perfect timing. She was faithful in her pursuit of knowledge and faithful in the way she managed and shared it. Her story is inspiring and applicable to us today.

Psalm 33 addresses those who sincerely seek God and aspire to please Him. It acknowledges His ultimate wisdom and authority and affirms that His plans are good. "The counsel of the Lord stands forever, the plans of His heart from generation to generation."[55] Esther provides an excellent example of being faithful with what we know. In this way, we can participate in His plan for people today and even in future generations.

GOD'S HAND OVER HIS PEOPLE

The setting for this biblical account is Persia, some one hundred years after Cyrus the Great conquered Babylon. The Persian Empire grew to be the most powerful and largest empire in the world. After the fall of Babylon, the Jews were free; their period of exile and slavery in Babylon was over. Cyrus was a shrewd ruler, realizing that benevolence toward the Jews would pay him in spades as he sought to enlarge his kingdom. Life was finally peaceful and promising, so most Jews opted to settle throughout the empire.

Diaspora originates from Greek and means a "scattering" or "dispersion" of a people.[56] The scattering began earlier in history when the Babylonian Empire had taken over Judah. Jews living in Judah were enslaved. A lack of faith and a desire for ease led the Israelites to stay put in Persia. For the Jews, not living in the Promised Land resulted in intermarriages and practicing the customs of their adopted homelands. The Diaspora was both the Israelites' disobedience and God's punishment.

In His lovingkindness, God did not forget His children. Rather than their annihilation, he made a way for their survival through Esther. She did not shape the politics of the day or

---

[55] v. 11 NASB.

[56] "Diaspora," Merriam-Webster.com, https://www.merriam-webster.com/dictionary/diaspora.

discuss battle plans with army generals. But she did not sit idly by, watching history unfold. She allowed God to use her for the good of her people. Her wise use of position and station in life inspires and applies to us today.

Esther's early life was tragic; she had been orphaned as a young girl after both parents died. An older unmarried cousin, Mordecai, finished raising her. How unusual to be in the care of a distant male relative. When other girls were braiding hair or learning to sew or kneading bread, Esther was probably immersed in Hebrew law, customs, and religion. Mordecai revealed himself as a person of faith, as did Esther. She cultivated an inner beauty that made her outer appearance even more striking.

The book of Esther begins with another strong and intelligent woman, Queen Vashti. King Xerxes, the grandson of Cyrus the Great, was the ruler of the Persian Empire. He hosted an elaborate six-month meeting with nobles and government officials to plan the battle and takeover of Greece, the only part of the world not in his kingdom. After the long meeting concluded, King Xerxes threw a seven-day party. The palace's decadence surpassed today's ritzy over-the-top hotels ... to the tenth power. We're talking ivory pillars, mosaic tiles of precious stones, and gold chalices from which to drink fine wine. He was ridiculously wealthy and that seven-day party was a lavish indulgence of epic proportions.

With his inhibitions at a low and the party at fever pitch, he sent for his queen. She was runway-model beautiful, the king's trophy wife. He sent seven eunuchs to carry her in, seated on a plush chair. It would be a grand entrance likely to invoke patriotism and loyalty. Queen Vashti knew her husband's propensity toward pretentiousness, so she figured her entrance would be for show. She also knew at the end of a weeklong celebration, she would be the only woman in a room full of intoxicated male government officials from every province in the kingdom. What was a woman to do?

She stood him up!

This left King Xerxes with only one choice, to strip Queen Vashti of her royalty. For Vashti, her crown was gone, but her dignity remained intact. For Xerxes, his act reinforced that women could not disrespect their husbands. It also reasserted the importance of loyalty to the king. The next order of business began—finding a new queen.

When King Xerxes' anger subsided, the royal servants began an early version of The Bachelor. Xerxes had a penchant for over-the-top opulence, so the process to find a new bride was extravagant. Scripture says, "As a result of the king's decree, Esther, along with many other young women, was brought to the king's harem at the fortress of Susa."[57]

Perhaps the girls had Cinderella dreams. Perhaps their fathers had ambitions of being in the king's inner circle. Nonetheless, a months-long beauty pageant ensued. It is unknown how Esther arrived, but she was among the hundreds of young women vying for the position of queen. Only she did not compete or contend; the Lord orchestrated.

The king's eunuch Hegai was put in charge of the spectacle. The women who met his approval were put in the king's harem. Then they engaged in twelve months of beauty treatments and preparations to go before the king. Esther found favor with Hegai. He gave her seven attendants and put her in the best place in the harem. There, she waited for her opportunity to meet the king.

Meanwhile, the battle to take Greece was a losing one. King Xerxes eventually returned to Susa, depressed and dismayed. And ready to meet his new queen.

He found Esther to be his cup of soothing tea. Beth Moore says Esther had developed people skills. "Never underestimate the impact of God-driven, Scripture-quickened people skills even in the most uncomfortable human encounters. We neither have to be carnal to be likable nor insincere to be endearing."[58]

---

[57] Esther 2:8 NLT.

[58] Beth Moore, *Esther, It's Tough Being a Woman* (Nashville: Lifeway Press, 2008), 41.

Indeed, her cultivated inner beauty made her incredible outer beauty that much more appealing.

Esther became Queen Esther. With this first incredible turn of events, her name proved prophetic. Queen Star. She had been placed in a position of prominence. She could hear the issues of the day and know people of importance. God, the silent character in this story, mingled in the background and set the stage for miraculous provision of his beloved Israelites.

OUR PLACE IN HISTORY

Esther's story, which reveals the challenge of discerning the moment to take destiny by the hand, is a call to refuse compliance and faithfully bear the truth.[59] While we are products of our generation, we choose whether we will be contributors to or consumers of our culture. We choose whether we will grab firmly to destiny or watch the sands of time slip through our fingers.

Our limited purview reveals only what we see around us and what we see today. God's infinite capacities reach beyond linear thought and constraints of time. He knows how our personal history prepares us for our destiny. He knows how our obedient action today will make a difference for eternity.

What if we could know how our involvement in a ministry could save souls and make innumerable impacts? What if our crazy business idea is precisely how God wants to use us for something greater, something with ripple effects we may not see until we reach heaven? Or what if our intervention in social problems or fracturing politics may create positive change? Will we be faithful with the little we know and trust God for the rest? Will we say yes to the challenge?

---

[59] Samuel Wells and George Sumner, *Esther and Daniel* (Grand Rapids: Baker Publishing Group, 2013), 23.

Sophie Scholl was a German college girl in the 1940s whose personal history served as preparation for her destiny. As a young girl, she was a member of the League of German Girls, a Nazi propaganda training program. Her enthusiasm waned as she looked deeper at the movement. As a student at the University of Munich, she was part of the same social circle as her brother and sister and others who were also critical of growing Nazism. The students discussed literature, art, history, politics, and theology and eventually called themselves the White Rose Society.

When they learned of German war crimes and mass killings of Jews, they chose passive resistance as their approach. Since the press was Nazi run, German citizens didn't know the truth. The White Rose Society opted to write anonymous letters outlining the atrocities they had discovered and used Scripture and philosophy in their appeal for public outcry.

To avoid being caught, writing and mailing quantities of letters required footwork. They purchased supplies in small batches from various locations. They secretly used a mimeograph in the middle of the night. Pamphlets were both mailed and left in public spots around campus. While distributing the fifth pamphlet, Sophie and her brother Hans were caught.

After a brief interrogation, one other member of the White Rose Society, Christoph Probst, was hauled in and then all three went before a stacked judge and jury. No defense was permitted. All three were found guilty of treason and sentenced to death by guillotine—that same day. It is said that her courage and strong faith in God deeply touched the prison guards.

Following their deaths, a sixth pamphlet was smuggled out of Germany and landed in the hands of Allied forces. In 1943, they dropped millions of pamphlets for Germans to read. It is now known as "The Manifesto of the Students of Munich." This remarkable story is depicted in the 2005 film *Sophie Scholl: The Final Days*.

This twenty-one-year-old college girl risked everything to inform her fellow countrymen of the truth. She was willing to step into the gap where common knowledge lacked. This is a somber reminder that our knowledge and life experience can be used by God for bigger things. Our faithfulness with the truth is part of God's infinite wisdom.

FAITHFUL BEARERS OF TRUTH

Both Queen Esther and Sophie Scholl acted upon the knowledge they acquired. Neither could see at the time how their contributions to the world were like a chapter in the grand book of history. The diaspora that began just a generation before Esther's promotion to queen involves us today. Jews scattered throughout the earth, from Babylonia, Syria, Asia Minor, and Egypt, then spreading years later throughout the Roman Empire, across Europe and Russia, into the United States during the immigration of the nineteenth century, and around the world.

As Jews spread throughout the earth, so has the meaning of *diaspora* changed. Christ is the fulfillment of the Law and the promise until the Law is fully accomplished.[60] And now anyone, whether Jew or Gentile, who believes in Christ as Savior is useful in God's grand design. In God's providence, the diaspora is beneficial to the advancement of the gospel. Believers in Christ throughout the world are called to participate in bringing people back to the Lord. In the figurative sense, we can guide others away from spiritual wandering and take them by the hand, back to the heart of God. Wherever we live and whatever era we live in, we can stake our lives upon the salvation of Christ. And we can lead others to do the same.

We may be called to change history. Or make a dent in our corner of the world. This much we know: we are called to be faithful with what we know to be true. What we know is but a spoonful of the depth of our all-knowing, all-powerful, ever-present holy God. Somehow, he takes our small acts and does something supernatural with them.

---

[60] See Matthew 5:17.

"I CAN HELP THEM THROUGH YOU"

Rachel is a wife and mother of two sons and a licensed clinical therapist. She worked part-time at a local agency serving children and teens with autism. When the state mandated changes to therapy programs like theirs, the agency owner assessed the numerous changes and decided to close. Rachel was concerned for her clients because changing therapists can be disruptive, even detrimental for children with autism. Soon to be out of a job, she figured there was not much she could do.

When two co-workers approached her with the idea of partnering together to open their own agency, her first response was, "No, thank you." Business ownership was not something that interested her. A couple of nights later, she had a dream. In it, the Lord challenged her, "You have an education and the experience. Are you going to walk away? What about these children?" She received the message loud and clear; the following day she spoke to her colleagues.

They had six weeks before the agency closed and their clients had to find other therapists. Out of a care for their clients' continuation of therapy, they were motivated to work fast. A big task was to find a psychologist who would align with their program, a necessity for state licensure. Rachel prayed about it, then proceeded to make cold calls. She easily found a psychologist who understood their philosophy of therapy and readily said yes. All of the state-required components simply fell into place. How they cut through governmental red tape in a matter of weeks was a miracle itself. But the story gets better.

Business grew exponentially because of the program's uniqueness and results. They eventually hired another therapist and divided the practice into two halves—autism and behavior disorders. Rachel focused on behavioral disorder cases. She routinely received calls about young people who were a step away from prison. These minors were violent, and many had lived through severe trauma. Time and again, Rachel prayed, "I can't do this," and in her spirit, she heard God answer, "I can help them through you."

With each client, Rachel visited the school and other key people and devised an individual plan. She creatively applied a strengths-based therapy approach and genuine care for each client. Six years later, all her initial clients have "aged out" of the program and they are doing well in life. The world had little hope for these kids. Rachel allowed the Lord to use her to make their lives better and show them love and concern. She was faithful with her education and experience. The Lord took it from there to transform the lives of these young people.

If we have an inkling, a leaning, a pull toward a vision for our lives, we can put it to an intelligence test. If our vision requires us to seek His Word and grow in character, and if our vision upholds the truth of the Word, then that is a beautiful vision to pursue. By faithfully sharing our knowledge, we can leave an imprint on others' lives. We can be a part of bringing people to the truth of God's Word. We can tell and show people they matter and they are loved. We can participate in God's greater plan.

QUESTIONS FOR REFLECTION

- In what ways does my vision draw me toward greater knowledge of the Word and a deeper relationship with God?

- Is there a need to develop expertise in my subject area? How can I be faithful sharing what I know?

- When do I know enough to start? If God is the expert, how can I be a willing worker?

7

Our Inadequacies Are Perfected in His Sufficiency

Esther 3–4

At one time or another, practically everyone struggles with feelings of inadequacy. Negative self-talk causes us to doubt and keeps us from pressing on.

When I was expecting my first son, I was uncertain that I could turn my part-time fun business into a full-time income. I did not have a long track record in sales and did not feel fully competent. After our son was born, I had no idea how I could care for a baby and a home-based business. I wanted the option of a flexible work-at-home lifestyle for our young family. And I was willing to try.

My husband and my mom were supportive and helped me in many ways. Steve loaded the car for my events and attended conferences with me. My mom started the practice of coming over once a week to stamp catalogs, stuff envelopes, and babysit while I worked.

I accepted their help and found that their actions spoke volumes. They loved me and wanted to see what this opportunity could do for me and our family. Their support helped me believe in my idea and achieve my goals in the long run.

People come into our lives for a reason, a season, or a lifetime. Scan the decades of our lives, and we find this saying accurate. Who has made a difference in your life? Who extended love and support and gave you the freedom to try something new—win or lose? That safety net makes all the difference.

As for Esther, it was Mordecai who played a significant role. He was both a loving adoptive parent and a beacon of truth. Mordecai prepared her for this experience in the palace. Then he offered urgent and important wisdom to do what seemed impossible.

A HORRIBLE FATE

After choosing Esther as his queen, King Xerxes made another decision. He elevated Haman from ordinary nobility to a seat of high honor. Everyone knelt to honor Haman, except Mordecai. When Haman discovered that Mordecai was a Jew, his annoyance quickly escalated to rage. Centuries earlier Mordecai's ancestors warred against Haman's. You could say Haman had a vendetta bubbling on the back burner. All it took was Mordecai the Jew not kneeling, and Haman's anger boiled.

Haman rolled the dice to select the exact month and day to exterminate Mordecai and all the Jews. He went before the king saying, "There is a certain people dispersed among the peoples in all the provinces of your kingdom who keep themselves separate. Their customs are different from those of all other people, and they do not obey the king's laws; it is not in the king's best interest to tolerate them. If it pleases the king, let a decree be issued to destroy them, and I will give ten thousand talents of silver to the king's administrators for the royal treasury."

So the king took his signet ring from his finger and gave it to Haman son of Hammedatha, the Agagite, the enemy of the

Jews. "Keep the money," the king said to Haman, "and do with the people as you please."

The decision was documented and communicated throughout the government and all the provinces. Then word got out among the commoners.

Mordecai revealed himself again as a man of faith. When he heard the news, he put on sackcloth and ashes to mourn. He went out to the city to weep and mourn but only got as far as the king's gate. When Esther's attendants saw Mordecai not looking well, they let her know. Esther called Hatak the messenger to inquire of Mordecai about his sad state. When Esther understood the story, this put her squarely between a rock and a hard place. The palace and its people did not know she was a Jew.

A flurry of messages went back and forth between Mordecai and Esther. Mordecai implored Esther to plead with the king for the lives of their people. Her predicament grew more uncomfortable. The king was a king, and anyone who went before him without being summoned risked their life. Unless the king wanted to hear from the uninvited guest, he or she would be put to death. The gold scepter had to be extended as a sign of his favor. How could Esther, even as his wife and as the queen, just sashay in?

RISE UP

Indeed, God speaks through His people to reach the heart. What followed was not only a key message in this story but sage advice for anyone facing a difficult decision. Mordecai sent back this message: "Do not think that because you are in the king's house you alone of all the Jews will escape. For if you remain silent at this time, relief and deliverance for the Jews will arise from another place, but you and your father's family will perish. And who knows but that you have come to your royal position for such a time as this?"

Slow down and listen. Mordecai did not mince words. Deliverance would come via some other means if Esther remained silent. She had a choice. Bury her head in the sand or pick up the hourglass and work with what remaining grains of sand were left. Let the fury of genocide sweep across the land or stand up and offer her own life if needed to save her people.

We must never take on the hopeless or prideful thought that it is all up to us. Both points of view are rooted in our selfishness and leave the Lord out of the equation.

As in Esther's story, God is in the midst of our unfolding stories. He orchestrates details and paves the way. He strongly supports us. He makes it easier for us to do hard things. But if we do not respond, rest assured he is working in the hearts of others. "God causes everything to work together for the good of those who love him and are called according to His purpose for them."[61] As for the Jews of Esther's day, God would save a remnant with or without Esther. He urged Esther as he does with us today, rise up.

Esther responded to this wise counsel in a God-honoring way: "Go, gather together all the Jews who are in Susa, and fast for me. Do not eat or drink for three days, night or day. I and my attendants will fast as you do. When this is done, I will go to the king, even though it is against the law. And if I perish, I perish."[62]

While Esther spoke of fasting, she was really talking about praying and fasting. The Hebrew custom always coupled the two. Esther rose to the occasion by dropping to her knees in prayer. During those three days, she found greater strength. With a calm demeanor bolstered by prayer, she took the hand of destiny.

On the third day, she approached the king, who not only extended his scepter but genuinely, perhaps warmly, asked, "What is it, Queen Esther? What is your request? Even up to half the kingdom, it will be given you." She opted for the tried-and-true getting to a man's heart through his stomach. She invited the king and Haman to dinner that evening.

---

[61] Romans 8:28 NLT.

[62] Esther 4:15.

When God's people pray, things happen.

At dinner that evening, the king kindly asked her, "Now what is your petition? It will be given you. And what is your request? Even up to half the kingdom, it will be granted." She responded with a request for a second dinner the next evening.

News of a second private dinner with the king and queen sent Haman over the top. He bragged to his friends and family about his rich and famous lifestyle. The only thing that would make his life better would be if Mordecai were not in it. His wife and friends suggested he construct a gallows from which to hang Mordecai. What a great idea! Haman strutted off to command his servants to build the death trap.

RECEIVING THE ROYAL SCEPTER OF GRACE

When you feel inadequate or incapable, pray. Invite the Lord in. When we offer our imperfect selves to God in prayer, he fills our less-than spaces with His grace. That is when things change, and God undeniably moves. Our successes can't possibly be ours alone under those circumstances. King Xerxes extended his scepter, and Esther simply reached out to receive his grace.

Just like Esther, we wear a royal robe. We are daughters of the King of kings. Yet we often cling to our desires. Our desire for safety and security, our desire to be right, our desire to do things our way, our desire to have what we want, and a thousand other desires we cling to. Like Esther, we have crossroads where we are confronted with choices. Once we let go of our way, we realize God's ways transcend our ways. Isaiah 55:9 says, "For just as the heavens are higher than the earth, so my ways are higher than your ways and my thoughts higher than your thoughts."[63]

Esther was no longer a young orphaned girl. She was queen and beloved by her king. Esther approached Xerxes and

---

[63] NLT.

received the royal scepter of God's love. With that came God's direction. And He shaped this story for good.

God is the silent character in our life stories as well. He crosses our paths with people who speak into our lives. He creates circumstances and cultivates hearts. He makes Himself known and His love palpable. When we receive His grace, our stories take a decidedly different turn. He offers His love, and we only need to say yes.

FROM INADEQUACY COMES SUFFICIENCY

Kim was once an overwhelmed mom of three. As a human resources executive on hiatus to raise her little boys, she was smack in the middle of the busy years. On top of that, her husband worked full-time and attended law school in the evenings. This meant Kim was alone with the children most of the time. With no easy way around their circumstances, they hoped things would ease up in a few years. Crafting a delicate plan of work-school-family-life was the easy part. It was the hours of time making peanut butter sandwiches, folding baskets of laundry, bathing children, and reading bedtime stories that brought her to a breaking point.

One evening after putting the boys down to bed, she went to the kitchen to wash dishes. Over a sink full of suds, the tears fell. Things were hard for Kim, but it was for a season and it was not without the love and support of a solid marriage. Even as she cried, the Lord spoke to her heart. "How do single moms do it?" she asked. In that raw moment, a heart for single moms was born.

From there, she contemplated her next move. The door flung open to graduate school. With a busy family life, it took six years to earn a master's degree in counseling psychology, but she had her eyes on the prize. She knew she wanted to serve single moms through social services and ministry. In the years that followed, she worked for a ministry to unwed pregnant women, then served as a counselor to low-income families at her large church, and she currently serves on the board of directors for a ministry to teen families.

From Kim's emptiness and exhaustion came a new purpose. Despite the need for an education to do what the Lord called her to do, he made a way. She reached out in sadness and the Lord met her there. He called her to new purpose. She speaks of her midlife career change with enthusiasm and gratefulness. Although it wasn't easy, there was joy because she was doing what the Lord called her to do.

If we are called to do something for God, it does not matter our age or experience. God is neither impressed by diplomas nor dismayed by a lack of experience. His grace is sufficient for all our inadequacies, inexperience, and uncertainties. We simply need to humbly accept what he offers. He who calls us is faithful; He will surely do it.[64]

❧

Sara grew up in the family business. Her mother was a financial advisor, and the family had several businesses, including a farm. From a young age, she was included in conversations about business and finances. She went on to receive a degree in marketing and desired to make her mark in the business world. While at a job fair, she made small talk with an insurance company representative while she waited for an interview with a marketing firm. She reluctantly agreed to sit for an interview with the insurance company, chalking it up to a "practice" interview.

That's when she realized her mother's career choice could be hers too. During the interview, she learned that much of what she wanted in life were perks of an insurance career. She could earn all-expense-paid pleasure trips, enjoy a flexible schedule, and get paid to give the advice she'd naturally and casually been giving for years. After taking the job and becoming a certified financial planner and insurance agent, she discovered even

---

[64] 1 Thessalonians 5:24 ESV.

greater significance. Serving in the area of personal finance is a calling for her. Sara says she is blessed to help people replace fear and anxiety with financial freedom and peace.

Launching her business in 2008 coincided with the Great Recession. She chose to grow her business through learning opportunities designed to impart hope. In 2009, she hosted her first conference especially for women. Her mission was to inspire and empower women to create financial peace of mind. The successful event continues today in various locations and reaches hundreds of women.

Perhaps Sara's greatest challenges and growth opportunities come from ownership of her business. Decisions about when to add staff and pay another salary are risks and leaps of faith. Hiring additional staff allowed the time to participate in a Bible study for business owners, something she wasn't fully aware she needed. There, she learned the benefit of iron sharpening iron. As a prominent business owner in her community, she is careful to remember that her true identity is God's daughter. Accepting the fellowship and support of a good Bible study and walking in step with the Lord allow her to lead her team and serve her clients from the fullness of God's love.

A HUMBLE YES

When we think we can't do something, we are right. We are empowered by the Holy Spirit, who makes us able. We are only able to go so far without the Lord. This is where humility comes in. Humility is the space between our hand and God's hand. Humility makes it possible for us to lift our hands in need and place them in God's good hand.

From orphaned girl to Queen of Persia and from secret Jew to harbinger heiress, Esther exemplified the right response to God's call. She chose to yield in humility. She understood her limitations in contrast to God's unlimited power, then wisely chose to accept God's love. She chose not to say, "I can't" but "God will." This is the way to say yes to God.

QUESTIONS FOR REFLECTION

- In what ways do I feel inadequate, unprepared, or uncertain?

- How has God shown Himself to be sufficient ... in the story of Esther and in my own life?

- What may happen if I humble myself and ask for and receive help?

8

Our Weakness Is His Strength

Esther 5–7

What a difference a day makes! Occasionally in life, we experience a turn of events resulting in a big change. After my first son was born, I could not bear the thought of putting him in daycare. I decided to turn my part-time business into a full-time income. Trouble was, the business was not generating the kind of income I needed. I took a month to recuperate and enjoy my newborn. Then, as the saying goes, I planned my work and worked my plan.

Sitting on the sofa holding my son, I made call after call. (Texting had not been "invented" yet!) I lined up ten selling events in one month, more than I had ever done. Estimating my sales, I realized that not only could I replace my income, but I could also earn a trip for two if I applied a bit more diligence. I created a fall kickoff campaign for my sales team to increase overall sales and recruiting.

The day finally came that we fully engaged our new plan. My husband got home from work, I put the baby in his arms, and I went out that evening for my first selling event. The results confirmed what I believed—my part-time business was going to make it. At the end of my first month back to business, my earnings matched my full-time pay. This quelled any fears of saying goodbye to my steady paycheck. I was officially a stay-at-home-mom, a dream come true! From that first selling party, everything changed for us.

A sudden turn of events can also be tragic. *Peripeteia* is a literary term for a sudden change in a story, a reversal of fortune. It is a turning point usually for the protagonist in a story, changing their circumstances from good to bad. Peripeteia is also meant to follow a character's previous actions or mistakes. Think of George Bailey of *It's a Wonderful Life*. At a point of desperation, George wished he'd never been born. His angel Clarence showed him a reversal of fortune, how horrible life would be for everyone without George. As we know, the story ends with a satisfying denouement as townspeople come to bail George out of a bad business deal and celebrate Christmas Eve.

A REVERSAL OF FORTUNE

Turning back to the story of Esther, a tragic reversal of fortune occurred for Haman. Because of his evil ways, he experienced a permanent reversal of fortune. In the span of twenty-four hours between Esther's two banquets, God brought Haman down.

The night between the two dinners, King Xerxes had trouble sleeping. He sent for a servant to read the royal record. He probably thought a reading of every detail in the kingdom would put him to sleep! Instead, his ears perked up when he heard that a plot to kill him had been prevented, by Mordecai no less. The royal record stated that some time earlier, Mordecai had heard two of the king's guards discuss assassination plans. He reported it, averted a crisis in the kingdom, and saved the king's life. King Xerxes asked, "What honor has been done for this man?" His attendants answered, "None."

Meanwhile, Haman was on top of the world. Everything was going his way. There was the upcoming extinction of the

Jews he hated, the gallows being erected to hang Mordecai, his luxurious home near the palace, dinners with the king and queen, friends, money, and fame. He arrived at the palace early that morning, loving life.

When King Xerxes asked him, "What should be done for the man the king delights to honor?," Haman naturally assumed the king was talking about him! Haman replied, "Bring a royal robe the king has worn and a horse the king has ridden, one with a royal crest placed on its head. Then let the robe and horse be entrusted to one of the king's most noble princes. Let them robe the man the king delights to honor, and lead him on the horse through the city streets, proclaiming, 'This is what is done for the man the king delights to honor!'"

The king then told Haman to go immediately and get the robe, the horse, and Mordecai. Certainly, Haman's smile turned upside down. And the blood probably drained from his face. And a knot formed in his stomach. As he led Mordecai around town on the king's horse, he could not have made the spectacle seem celebratory. Not only was his heart not in it, he was also worried sick about his predicament. At home later that day, his friends and family spoke of his doom. Before he had a chance to come up with a plan B, the king's eunuchs arrived to take him to his second dinner with the king and queen.

At dinner, the king asked Esther the same question as the night before: "Tell me what you want, Queen Esther. What is your request? I will give it to you, even if it is half the kingdom!"[65] Esther replied with the same respect she'd used the night before:

"If I have found favor with you, Your Majesty, and if it pleases you, grant me my life—this is my petition. And spare my people—this is my request. For I and my people have been sold to be destroyed, killed, and annihilated. If we had merely been sold as male and female slaves, I would have kept quiet, because no such distress would justify disturbing the king."[66]

---

[65] Esther 7:2 NLT.
[66] vv. 3–4.

Xerxes demanded an answer. "Who would do such a thing? … Who would be so presumptuous as to touch you?" Esther answered, "An adversary and enemy! This vile Haman!" The king left the table in a rage. Haman made himself look even worse, falling on the queen and begging for his life as she reclined on the sofa. The king saw this and exclaimed, "Will he even assault the queen right here in the palace, before my very eyes?"[67]

Palace guards threw a cover over Haman's face to take him to his death. One of the eunuchs let the king know about the seventy-five-foot-high gallows next to Haman's home. The gallows for Mordecai was instead used for Haman.

Talk about a reversal of fortune. That morning, Haman was on top of the world. That evening, his body lay beneath the dirt. What a difference a day can make.

This story hinges upon that twenty-four-hour period. What might have happened if Esther had pleaded for her people at the first dinner? Would Haman have twisted the king's point of view to his favor? Was Esther sickened in the presence of Haman? Would her voice have trembled? Was she angry and would she have said regrettable things? She may have wanted Haman's head more than the deliverance of an entire people. While we do not know exactly why she requested a second banquet, we do see the benefits of just a bit more time to let things develop. God orchestrated this incredible story.

In her solitary effort to save her people, she remained measured and respectful in her dealings with King Xerxes. All she could do was stand in her meager strength—just one woman. It was God who brought things to a head. In her humanness, her weakness, God was certainly strong.

BUILDING COURAGE

"Take heart." That's what we often say when we want to boost a burdened friend. What we're really saying is "Find your courage."

---

[67] v. 5 NLT, v. 6, v. 8 NLT.

Interestingly, courage comes from the Latin root word *cor*, which also means heart.[68] Courage comes from the heart. From the heart, otherwise known as the soul, we think, feel, and choose. Our souls pivot our lives; within our souls we respond and make our choices. Courage grows when we choose to grow it. Esther grew her courage when she fasted and prayed. When we wait upon the Lord, some incredible benefits derive. First, we gain a new strength and a fresh perspective on the situation. Things tend to look better in the morning. And some miraculous things may occur during our fallow hours. During our waiting, we store up energy for the eventual task ahead of us and we deepen our determination to press on.[69]

Bravery is the ability to confront danger or a difficult task without fear and typically with quick action. Courage is the ability to take on an overwhelming task despite an accompanying fear. To act courageously is a choice. We grow our inner courage muscles by choosing to pray and waiting upon the Lord.

IN OUR WEAKNESS, HIS POWER IS MADE PERFECT

After a satisfying career in direct sales, I made the transition from direct sales leader to my independent coaching and training business. Just as that business was hitting its stride, my husband's cancer returned. I juggled client appointments around frequent long and serious doctor appointments. Then things quickly went from bad to worse, and Steve was admitted to the hospital for a week of emergency chemotherapy. I arranged for my mother-in-law to stay with the kids so I could stay one hour away at the hospital.

At night, I slept on a cot in Steve's private hospital room. In the mornings, I was present when the medical team made their rounds. During the day, I found quiet alcoves around the hospital complex to manage calls with clients.

---

[68] "Courage." Merriam-Webster.com, https://www.merriam-webster.com/dictionary/courage.

[69] Charles R. Swindoll, *Esther: A Woman of Strength and Dignity* (Nashville: Thomas Nelson, 1997), 108.

One day, I asked the nurses if I could work in their conference room. I had to finish preparing a webinar for a group of clients that evening. My husband suffered down the hall receiving chemo while I feverishly worked at my computer. Everything about it seemed wrong. After teaching the webinar that night, I returned to Steve's hospital room exhausted, too tired to talk to him and offer moral support.

The most horrible year of our life followed that emergency seven-day stretch in the hospital. It was one thing after another, as late-stage cancer goes. With a very sick husband and three school-aged kids, there was nothing else I could do (or wanted to do) but care for them.

One by one, I let clients go.

Occasionally I would question: *Did I get the timing wrong for this business venture? Will I go back to it? What was the point of all this?*

My husband received the ultimate healing of heaven after a hard-fought battle. After his passing, I formally closed my business. Exhausted and with three kids to care for, I knew we simply needed to grieve and heal.

Would I ever be in business again? Did my dream die along with my beloved?

I did not have the answers; I could only lay my questions at the Lord's feet. I truly had no idea when I would be ready to work and what that work would be.

Over time, the gray clouds of grief dissipated. The sun shone rays of hope. I looked ahead to new dreams more than I looked back at memories. With a deepened perspective, I found the courage to begin again.

Mixing my business background with my earnest desire to see women flourish and serve God, I began coaching entrepreneurial Christian women. Guiding women through business strategy to reach their full potential is gratifying.

I see now that my former coaching business was useful training. God's timing is perfect.

COURAGE—A DECISION FROM THE HEART

In times of uncertainty and in our weakest moments, God makes Himself undeniably present. During the hard episodes of life, He is our good Father. He comforts, yes. And when the time is right, He challenges us to gather our courage.

Take heart!

Joshua was called to lead the Israelites out of Canaan and to the Promised Land, despite the dangers and battles. God promised to be with Joshua but also commanded him to keep the Law. The Israelites needed spiritual and physical strength for the charge ahead. After Moses' death, the Lord told Joshua:

> "Be strong and courageous, for you are the one who will lead these people to possess all the land I swore to their ancestors I would give them. Be strong and very courageous. Be careful to obey all the instructions Moses gave you. Do not deviate from them, turning either to the right or to the left. Then you will be successful in everything you do. Study this Book of Instruction continually. Meditate on it day and night so you will be sure to obey everything written in it. Only then will you prosper and succeed in all you do. This is my command—be strong and courageous! Do not be afraid or discouraged. For the Lord your God is with you wherever you go."[70]

After this prayerful dialogue with God, how did Joshua respond? Without hesitation and with courage.

He ordered his officers to get ready and gather the people. He then addressed the Israelites with the plan to leave Jericho against the odds and cross the Jordan.

The people responded with their allegiance to Joshua. The battle of Jericho followed soon after, and as that old children's song goes, the walls came tumbling down. God's show of strength was undeniable. The Israelites marched around the

---

[70] Joshua 1:6–9 NLT.

walled city each day for seven days, then blew a ram's horn, gave a shout, and the walls crumbled.

Ultimately, the Israelites' passage from Jericho across the Jordan and into all of Canaan was a symbolic salvation and an example of victorious living.

From Joshua to Esther throughout the pages of Scripture and in our own lives, time and again, human weakness gives rise to courage. Following God ultimately requires us to submit our human frailties and gather the cords of spiritual fiber. Never leaving or forsaking us, God meets our courage with His strength.

Dear one, entrust your meager efforts to His might. Our vision and our whole lives are clearer and firmer standing in His strength.

QUESTIONS FOR REFLECTION

- Has there been a reversal of fortune in my life? Jesus Christ is the Redeemer. Have I asked for redemption of my soul and my life circumstances?

- What have I pursued for my glory? How did that turn out? What will I pursue for God's glory?

- God wants to do something in me and through me. How can I develop greater courage to face my challenges?

9

Our Lack Is God's Abundance

Esther 8–10

According to polls, as many as seven out of ten Americans have thought about starting their own business at one time or another.[71] Yet according to Gallup, only 10 percent of all working adults are self-employed; a smaller subset of 4 percent have small businesses with employees.[72]

Why do so few pursue their entrepreneurial dreams?

With business failure rates as high as 50 percent, certainly would-be business owners have reason for pause. Among the top reasons for business failure is lack of funds.[73] Typically, personal savings provide initial funding for a business start-up. From there, a small business needs to quickly acquire contracts

---

[71] Peter Economy, "Want to Start a Home-Based Business?," *Inc.*, July 20, 2017.
[72] David W. Moore, "Majority of Americans Want to Start Own Business," GALLUP, April 12, 2005.
[73] Sangeeta Bharadwaj Badal and Bryant Ott, "Many Potential Entrepreneurs Aren't Taking the Plunge," GALLUP, February 18, 2015.

and bring in sales to stay afloat and scale. These financial facts often keep people from pursuing their dream.

If money were no object, would the drive to succeed become obsolete? Would the dream business sputter and die?

Money makes the world go around. We would be wise to acknowledge the source of abundance. God is the source of every resource. Just as marvelous as God's original genius is His personal love. He generously, richly gives what we need at the right time, in the perfect way, and for purposes beyond our comprehension.

VICTORY AND CELEBRATION

When we first met Esther, she was a simple, God-honoring young woman. Courage grew in her heart, enabling her to save her people even at the risk of her own life. Neither reckless nor foolish, Esther was prayerful and careful. The willingness to do what it takes to accomplish our most important callings is the spark that burns our visions bright.

After Haman was executed, Esther received his estate from King Xerxes. She had proven herself to be trustworthy and prudent. She appointed Mordecai over the estate, and the king gave Mordecai his signet ring. Still, the previous decree to kill the Jews had to be cancelled.

Esther fell at the king's feet and wept, pleading to him, "How can I bear to see disaster fall on my people? How can I bear to see the destruction of my family?"

The king wrote another decree giving the Jews the right to assemble and protect themselves against enemies if warranted. Now the king's right-hand man, Mordecai, wore a royal robe, a crown, and a signet ring on his finger. The king's decree was sealed by Mordecai's ring, then the news rushed out by horsemen across the land. A celebration broke out in the city of Susa. After fasting and praying for days, the Jews feasted joyfully.

On the prearranged date according to Haman's original decree, fighting broke out. The Jews struck their enemies by sword. In Susa alone, five hundred enemies were killed, including Haman's ten sons. The king asked Queen Esther for her petition. She requested one more day of fighting and to impale Haman's sons. Across the kingdom, more than seventy-five thousand enemies of the Jews were killed.

Afterward, Esther requested a two-day feast. It became an annual celebration for every province and every family to observe a joyful remembrance of their deliverance. The feasting would be a reminder of the fasting, praying, and grief the Jews experienced before they were miraculously and mightily saved.

The celebration, Purim, is still observed by Jews today. Purim is plural for *pur*, which means "lot," as in casting lots. *Pur* has a second meaning: "destiny." Instead of allowing evil men to play a game of chance with their lives, God protected His people. Instead of sitting idly by, together they stepped into their destiny.

King Xerxes was won over by Esther's beauty, faith, and demeanor. But it was God who worked this episode of history together for good. Esther began this chapter in her life prepared for the task, yet this challenge provided a huge spiritual growth opportunity. She leaned into the learning and developed her character and her faith. In the end, God rewarded Esther and Mordecai by raising them to positions of honor.

LIVING FROM BLESSING

In our culture, we've come to expect success after sacrifice. We tend to think in an if-then fashion. If we do what God wants, then we will be rewarded. If we serve or give, then it will be multiplied. If we give up something or change or let go, it will be reclaimed.

Could it be that we've become infatuated with our lives, this world, and what we see? As fallen people, have we fallen for the passing charms of this world?

Oh, that our hearts would fall in love with the grace of God and the beauty of the cross. We ought to live our lives from blessing, not for it. Jon Tyson perfectly states this in his book *The Burden Is Light*:

> The last thing the disciples saw before Jesus ascended into heaven was Him raising His hands and blessing them. What a beautiful sight! As they went on with their ministry, they understood the proper relationship between ministry and blessing. All ministry flows from blessing, not for it. We minister because we are blessed, not to gain blessing.[74]

Living from joy and living for our upcoming innumerable and incomprehensible joys of heaven is the only way to live.

A BUSINESS FROM BLESSING

Sisters Ashley and Taylor took their first entrepreneurial steps as seventh- and tenth- grade students. They developed an app, a cross between a game and social media. With their parents' help, they worked with a marketing company to launch the app. The consultants took the girls under their wing and taught them about internet marketing. The girls had many interests, including video-making, fashion, cooking, photography, and music. They were also sincere young believers. At the suggestion of the marketing consultants, they started a YouTube channel to promote the app and grow the business.

The app never gained traction and took off. At the same time, the girls grew tired of making videos that talked of teenage interests devoid of biblical truth. So they shut it down. While most people fear failure, Ashley and Taylor laugh at the app failure and quickly credit God for the journey. Their entrepreneurial attempts brought them to their current ministry-related business, Coffee and Bible Time. They retooled their message to put God first. Through videos, social media, a website, and products, they appeal to creative young women with heartfelt conversation about the Bible and the Christian life.

At seventeen and twenty years of age, they are at the life stage of choosing colleges and careers. A certified beautician, Ashley had been training to take her skills to the mission field. In preparation for a six-month leave, the girls created dozens of

---

[74] Jon Tyson, *The Burden Is Light* (New York: Multnomah, 2018), 97.

weekly videos. They scheduled their weekly posts and walked away for an extended leave. Ashley attended missionary training while Taylor returned to school, completing eleventh and twelfth grades in one school year. An astonishing thing happened while they focused on other important goals: their followership grew exponentially. This opened their eyes to see Coffee and Bible Time as God's plan for them.

The girls say Coffee and Bible Time exists to make God's name known, spread the gospel, and disciple young believers. While they have goals and work hard on the business, they have dedicated it all to God. They choose to be faithful with what he has called them to do today.

IMMEASURABLY MORE—THE HOPE OF HEAVEN

Yes, God can take our little idea and bring forth seed money or make a video go viral or bring us our next big break. He is able to do immeasurably more than all we can ask or imagine because he holds every resource under heaven. It is important to remember that he provides for us not only for this lifetime. He also holds every resource in heaven as well, and a glorious future is waiting for us.

Paul's letter to the Ephesians reveals the beauty and mystery of heaven and our purpose in God's great plan. We are not only saved for our personal benefit. We are saved to bring glory to God. This prayer from Paul is for us today, as well.

> I pray that out of his glorious riches he may strengthen you with power through his Spirit in your inner being, so that Christ may dwell in your hearts through faith. And I pray that you, being rooted and established in love, may have power, together with all the Lord's holy people, to grasp how wide and long and high and deep is the love of Christ, and to know this love that surpasses knowledge—that you may be filled to the measure of all the fullness of God. Now to him who is able to do immeasurably more than all we ask or imagine, according to his power that is at work within us, to

him be glory in the church and in Christ Jesus throughout all generations, for ever and ever! Amen.[75]

Living by vision reveals our true nature—that eternity is written on our hearts. Living by vision requires character development. Living by vision aligns us to God's Word and shapes us into a closer image of Christ. Vision is future focused and hopeful. It prepares us for heaven. God uses it for divine purposes. From the moment we receive Christ as our Savior, the sanctification process begins and does not stop until we reach heaven. Vision guides us to our destination.

I have often contemplated that we take nothing with us when we depart for heaven. Except what is tucked in our souls. Living by vision requires us to grow in Christlikeness. Those character qualities we cultivate stay with us. The ways we serve and the things we did for Christ and the Scripture we know are tucked away inside. Those are the things we will lay at the throne, where every knee will bow and every tongue confess that Jesus is Lord. What a celebration it will be! Like Esther and the Jews of Susa celebrating their deliverance at Purim, we will celebrate our deliverance from sin through this life and to eternal life.

LIVING FOR GOD'S GLORY

Leonid and Elo are a semi-retired missionary couple of Russian descent. They had similar childhood experiences—each was bravely led out of Communist Russia by their parents. Years later, after meeting and marrying, and still overcome with gratitude for their freedom, they dedicated their lives to ministry. They were compelled to share the gospel with those living in the religion-stripped oppression of communism.

Over the span of thirty-plus years, they served in South Korea and Ecuador, broadcasting Leonid's sermons via short-wave radio to unreached corners of the world. It is impossible to know how many souls have come to Christ through their

---

[75] Ephesians 3:16–21.

radio ministry. Leonid studied and prepared his daily message while Elo assisted with the broadcast. Together they responded to the constant flow of correspondence from listeners who did not have Bibles or churches but had a hunger for God.

They partnered with a missionary organization, lived frugally, and trusted God to meet their needs. Their years on the mission field included countless moves, and each residence came with whatever furniture was (or was not) there. During the last decade of their ministry, they were stationed in Russia, where the apartments were especially sparse. One place they lived didn't have a refrigerator—a challenge for a woman who loves to cook! They found ways to lovingly transform each address into a home.

Elo's greatest sacrifice in ministry was the years their sons attended college stateside. Each time she left an incoming freshman son on campus and boarded a plane back to Ecuador, she left a piece of her heart a continent away. Back home, she did what came naturally—making boxes of homemade goodies and shipping them to her boys' dorm room doorsteps. And she prayed for them daily. For her, food and prayer are expressions of love.

As an international family, it was anybody's guess where they'd all end up. But God knew! One by one, each son graduated and settled in the States. Eventually Leonid and Elo relocated to the U.S. and retired from mission work but not from ministry. Their consistent and loving presence in each son's family is now their ministry. This large extended family remains remarkably close because of their shared love of the Lord and because Leonid and Elo tangibly demonstrate love. Whether it is filling in for the car pool, trimming hedges and planting roses, taking care of grand-dogs, or cooking an abundance of food to deliver to their kids' doors, this couple sets an example of devotion.

They did not dream of riches or fame; they dedicated their lives to the Lord's work and hoped to grow old with their family around them. They are flourishing.

Psalm 92 says, "Even in old age they will still produce fruit; they will remain vital and green."[76] Leonid and Elo are living out their retired years still producing fruit. This delightful couple views their daily activities as a service to God. From preaching the gospel to multitudes to sweet conversations with immediate family, they are building the kingdom and fulfilling God's vision for their lives.

HEAVEN'S INCOMPARABLE RICHES

Any worthy vision carries some risk. That's the point. Vision calls us forth.

Will we drop to our knees in surrender? Will we share what we know faithfully? Will we lift our hand in humility? Will we receive the royal scepter of our King's great love? Will we act with courage? Will we look at our future with hope?

Dear one, the richness he offers makes following our dreams even more adventuresome. Grab the hand of destiny, live in light of heaven, say yes, and go!

QUESTIONS FOR REFLECTION

- Have I loved this world more than the next? Have I loved my life more than Christ's sacrifice for my life?

- Read Ephesians 3:16–21 once again. Considering this passage, what does living from blessing, not for blessing, mean?

- What holds me back from fully embracing God's call?

---

[76] v. 14 NLT.

10

Long-Range Vision

Many summers ago, my family toured the National Museum of the U.S. Air Force in Ohio. Honestly, spending a day touring hangars and viewing countless aircraft was my husband's idea, not mine. Nonetheless, the collection of Orville and Wilbur Wright artifacts captured my imagination. Their audacious vision gave them the nerve to strap themselves into primitive gliders when the idea of air flight was considered far-fetched by everyone else. After years of experimentation, Orville Wright piloted the first powered flight at Kitty Hawk Beach in 1903. It lasted fifty-nine seconds and travelled 852 feet. Small beginnings, indeed! Today, we can travel anywhere thanks to the Wright brothers' tenacity.

Our dreams are limited only by our imaginations. Ascending mountain peaks, taking flight, sailing the seas, reaching personal bests, serving God in far-flung places, leaving a job and starting a business ... are all worthy dreams. Yet our highest heights can never surpass God's greatness. Whatever we dare dream, His love is greater still. It is guiding and lighting our way. It is hemming us in and conforming us to His Son. It is grounding us in wisdom and keeping us humble. It is both comforting in hard times and cheering us in the races. His banner over us is love.

Thirty years ago, I had a dream. Well, I backed into it. But I had a dream all right. As a high school senior, I shocked my mother when I declared theater as my college major. It was the furthest thing from her mind that I would pursue my fun activity past high school graduation. After a couple of years of her discontent, I acquiesced and changed majors from theater to public relations to creative writing to education. Then I lost my way, and I dropped out of school. I came home and got a job as an administrative assistant. Not my dream job, but it was a paycheck.

One mind-numbing afternoon while transcribing letter after letter, I wondered if I had made a big mistake. I decided I would spend my evening praying, reading the Bible, journaling, and finding the answers I desperately desired. That afternoon, I had no idea what I wanted to do with my life. But I determined I would go to bed knowing.

By 11:00 p.m., I had come up with nothing.

Disappointed, I slumped over and prayed, "Lord, I still have no idea about my life. But I have this desk job to go to in the morning. I have to get some sleep."

In the middle of the night, I had a vivid dream. I was on the stage of the fellowship hall of my childhood church. A room full of women were listening to me talk because I had authored a book. Completely surprised, this jarred me awake.

"Lord, I am nineteen years old. What have I got to say? How can this be?"

As I rolled over to try to sleep again, I felt a calm.

What came over me was, "Give it time."

☙

Vision has compelled me over the years. Just like I prayed for Cami, Katie, and Kathleen many years ago, I pray for my clients today. I still have a vision board, but my desires have changed.

And so has the way I use my vision board.

Nowadays, it's a motivating tool and display of artwork. It also provides a fun way to pray over my hopes and dreams. My vision board has pictures of happy-looking work-at-home women alongside pictures of ministries where I serve and give and where I want to contribute. And pictures of Italy. I can't get Tuscany out of my head, so I put it on my vision board.

PATIENCE SERVES A PURPOSE

As we learned from Abraham's story, vision is a lifetime process. In our sound-bite world, we want immediate gratification, no waiting required. Alas, patience is a virtue. With time comes character building. Consider it training.

Patience can be a bitter pill or a balm. When we're frustrated that things take time and work, energy, and investment, it's a tough realization, a bitter pill. Alternatively, we can choose to accept the process and give our circumstances over to God. We can relax and trust God's leading, a balm for the weary soul. Choose patience. Making things happen is not better than letting things happen. Bitter pill or healing balm, we choose which way to apply patience to our vision.

We can wait with gladness for God's perfect timing. We can take steps forward following the light our vision provides. While we wait patiently, there are two things we can do: pray and learn. Pray for God's leading. Pray Scripture. Pray for opportunities to arise.

God's Word will never return void, and time spent in prayer will always benefit us. We build character when we allow God to shape us into the likeness of His Son. We become trustworthy with bigger things when we honor the daily things of life.

We can also learn more about things that relate to our vision. If you want to write a book, start blogging or writing articles. If you believe God is calling you to start a ministry, then begin serving in a similar capacity. If you want to start a business, begin learning about running a business. Read books on your topic, meet experts, take seminars, and grow your list of professional contacts.

Learning about our areas of interest eventually results in expertise. It may take years for God's perfect timing to reveal itself, but if we aren't engaged on some level, we won't recognize opportunities when they arrive.

God gave Abraham a vision that nations of people would be his lineage and legacy. His lifetime of faithfulness was richly rewarded. One of the stars in the sky would be Esther, who also listened to the Lord's leading and saved her people. Her years of preparation met with a moment of courage. And Esther's story overlapped in the history books with Zerubbabel, a faithful man who also answered God's call and lived by an extraordinary vision.

The Jews' elaborate temple, also known as King Solomon's Temple, had been ransacked and destroyed when Nebuchadnezzar besieged Jerusalem. After seventy years of political division, warring, and turmoil which included the Jews' captivity in Babylon, Cyrus the Great of Persia conquered Babylon. He restored a measure of civility and kindly allowed the Jews to rebuild the temple. Cyrus the Great was the great-grandfather to King Xerxes. Under Persian reign, the Jews found favor.

After all those years of the Israelites being temple-less, Zerubbabel took up the charge to rebuild the temple. It was the center of Jewish life and crucial to their cultural and spiritual identity. The holy of holies resided there, temple priests performed sacrifices and prayers on the altar, and rites and festivals took place in and around the temple. As the work was about to begin, the Lord said to him, "Do not despise these small beginnings, for the Lord rejoices to see the work begin, to see the plumb line in Zerubbabel's hand."[77]

To build the temple, many tools were needed. Perhaps the most important was the plumb line held vertically from Zerubbabel's hand and pointing northward to heaven. The Lord had the blueprint for the temple, for each human heart, and for our lives today. The importance of the work surpassed the temple

---

[77] Zechariah 4:10 NLT.

itself. The state of our hearts is more important than the building where our hearts worship.

Yet the temple holds major significance. It is tied to end times and the church universal. The temple was also the place where the veil was torn when Jesus died, signifying Jesus as the one and only atoning sacrifice. He is the bridge between the sinful soul of man and the perfection of God, the holy of holies. Zerubbabel could not have fully understood the significance of laying brick upon brick. His work contributed toward a vision far greater than his eye could see.

God's story continues from the pages of Scripture through the pages of today's history books and the pages of our own lives. His story will continue onward until the end of the age. And so we can learn to delight in our small beginnings and simple steps. Dear one, live in anticipation and with open hands. Just continue walking toward your full potential in Christ.

∽

The hymn "Be Thou My Vision" was written in the sixth century by Irish poet and monk Dallan Forgaill. He was a zealous lover of words, and it is believed that his long hours of reading and study contributed to his eventual loss of eyesight, which is what inspired this poem.

Upon its completion, Irish monks included the sixteen poetic verses in their prayers and incantations. In the early nineteen hundreds, the prayer received new life. It was translated into English and eventually set to an ancient Irish melody. It appeared in an Irish hymnbook in 1919, then became a popular hymn in England. Finally, the hymn was discovered by American hymnbook publishers after World War II and became a beloved hymn in American church worship.

Imagine Forgaill at a humble wooden writing desk, putting plume to papyrus and crafting a prayer. In poetry, he poured his heart out to God as his eyesight was fading: "Be Thou my vision, O Lord of my heart. Naught be all else to me, save that

Thou art. Thou my best thought, by day or by night. Waking or sleeping, Thy presence my light."

Forgaill looked upon his condition with courage and chose to see with the eyes of his heart. He reaffirmed his faith and praised the Lord despite his coming days of darkness. Fifteen hundred years later, his words still draw people to worship and bring glory to God. He could never have known his private prayer would endure through the ages.

But God knew. God's vision is greater.

God's vision is having a relationship with every man, woman, boy, and girl. His vision is walking with us from the cross where we find Christ to the throne where we will see Him in glory. And everything between those two points is laden with His love. Hold to that vision. Amen.

QUESTIONS FOR REFLECTION

- The Wright brothers were enthralled by flight, and their vision to fly lit the runway of their lives. What is my audacious vision—my BHAG (big holy audacious goal)?

- How can I apply patience and not be passive toward my vision becoming reality in my life?

- What steps am I going to take now to live my vision and God's calling for me? Write it down and commit. It's time to start!

Summary of *VISION* in Pictures

 Sow the seeds of obedience to God, compassion for others, and confidence in the Word.

 Choose from the soul, which is one's emotions, will, and intellect.

 Grab the hand of destiny. Our obedient action today makes a difference for eternity.

 Our intelligence is found in His ultimate wisdom. Be faithful with truth and knowledge.

 Our inadequacies are perfected in His sufficiency. Humbly reach for help and accept its gifts. The King's scepter is extended in love.

 Our weakness is His strength. Courage is a decision from the heart. It is the ability to take on overwhelming tasks despite any fear.

 Our lack is His abundance. Hope is the key to unlock our limited view and see that anything is possible.

 We were made with eternity in mind and have an inner desire to please God.

BONUS GUIDE #1

How to Host Vision Board Parties and Workshops

For Coaches, Small Group Leaders,
Women's Ministry Coordinators, and Girlfriends

For several years, Sabrina and April have co-led a women's Bible study at their church. Every January, the ladies create small vision boards to fit an eight-by-ten-inch picture frame. They spend an evening talking about their hopes and goals for the year and how they hope to grow in their faith, then they cut out magazine pictures. Each woman takes her frame home to pray about it, think about it, and see how God moves.

As a single mom, Sabrina does all she can for her son and does not indulge her own desires very often. So when she put together her first vision board, she posted two material items, an Apple watch and a bright blue bike with a basket for riding back and forth to the farmer's market. These were fun add-ons to more noble pictures of mission trips she wants to take (and she's already gone around the world on many). She didn't put as much emphasis, thought, or prayer into the material desires and put more prayer emphasis on the mission trip she was leading.

Months later, a friend mentioned that she wanted to let go of her brand-new bike; it wasn't exactly what she wanted. Interestingly, it was the identical bike to the one in Sabrina's picture! When Sabrina asked how much her friend wanted for it, the friend let it go for a fraction of the original price. An easy check to write!

Because Sabrina's vision board was in a picture frame and placed on her night table, her family knew what her dreams were. They took notice of her dreams and goals. That year at Christmas, her family went in together on a group gift—an Apple watch. Just as the year was coming to a close, everything she dreamed of came to be.

Reflecting on this exercise, Sabrina shared how God loves to give gifts and surprise us. "If it's important to you, it's important to Him," she said. "Put it down [on your vision board]. God showed me through this that He cares about the details, as if He is speaking the words 'I love you.'"

One of the small group members shared that she capably, easily manages her home and the revolving door of busy family life. She cut out a picture of a confident and peaceful-looking woman. She wanted to feel as confident in the Word as she was managing her home. She decided to be spiritual healthy and began a year of growing closer to the Lord. This is an excellent application for a vision board!

April, the Bible study co-leader, wanted a new job. Once she put that on her vision board, she got into action by updating her resume and beginning a job search. Indeed, she got a nice step up with a new employer. One could say it was simply a decision made that resulted in action and results. But any praying person knows that God directs our paths and guides our steps. April said, "Our lives are bigger than our circumstances." She shared that her job search experience drew her closer to the Lord, and she gives God the glory for her new position in life.

These women reveal the power of a group. From the energy and enthusiasm of a new idea and a fun experience to the ongoing friendship and prayer support, a group holds one another accountable. Once we share a dream or a goal with others, we increase the potential of achievement. This creates new neuropathways in the brain! Christian women also spur one another on in the faith, keeping us close the One who has every resource to bring about our visions. This strengthens our spiritual muscles in preparation for the moment we arrive at our desired destination in life.

✑

During the 1930s and 1940s, there was a group of British male friends known as the Inklings. Instructors affiliated with Oxford University and lovers of literature, they met weekly to discuss literary works and critique one another's writings. Nineteen members in all produced hundreds of journal articles, poems, scholarly texts, and fantastical nonfiction. This group changed the direction of one another's lives and made a significant literary impact.

The two most notable members of the group were C. S. Lewis and J. R. R. Tolkien. Initially, Tolkien was a mentor to Lewis, encouraging him in his writing and his faith. Tolkien played a major role in Lewis's spiritual journey from doubt to belief. But after Lewis's writing career took off, he was the one who spurred on Tolkien's long quest to complete his most famous work. The gap between the publication of *The Hobbit* and *The Lord of the Rings* spanned approximately fifteen years. In an interview to promote the newly published *Lord of the Rings*, Tolkien said of Lewis, "Only by his support and friendship did I ever struggle to the end of the labour."[78]

---

[78] Michael Hyatt, *Your Best Year Ever* (Grand Rapids, MI: Baker Books, 2018), 179.

The Inklings challenged and supported one another. They formed bonds among fellow kindred spirits, just as "iron sharpens iron."[79] Those men made one another better writers and achieved great professional heights. Moreover, they became better people and followers of Christ through their friendship.

We need each other. To fulfill our mission, live out our vision, and become more of the person we are meant to be, we need each other. That's why creating your vision board is better done with others.

Crystallize your calling and share it with those who will care. Then watch what God does.

These final pages contain the steps for a Vision Board Workshop that benefits you and blesses others. Consider this your call to action. It's time to stop reading and start doing!

PRAY

Commit to the Lord whatever you do, and he will establish your plans.

PROVERBS 16:3

- Commit your vision board workshop to the Lord. Ask Him to guide your steps and lead the right people to this and bless your time.

- Ask Him to continue showing you His vision and His desires for your life. Ask that you will listen and yield to Him.

- Pray that your will surrenders to His will and that your will becomes His will.

- Pray the Lord will prepare the hearts of the people who will attend the vision board workshop.

---

[79] Proverbs 27:17.

- Pray the workshop would be any of the following: fun, positive, supportive, meaningful, honest, motivating, prayerful, social, exciting.

- Pray that participants come ready to make their vision boards and share their hopes and dreams.

- Pray the workshop will draw others closer to the Lord.

PLAN

- Where will you hold your workshop? Location is important because table space or floor space is needed to make vision boards. Good lighting is also important. Include details on location in the invitation.

- Consider charging a per person materials fee. Include this in the invitation.

- Collect magazines. Request from friends via social media. Make certain you have a variety, including fashion and beauty, home décor, travel, cooking, Christian, hobby, and general women's interest magazines.

- How will you create the vision boards? Will pictures be mounted in notebooks, large or small poster boards, or put into a picture frame?

- Other supplies needed: one pair of scissors for each attendee, double stick tape, good quality glue sticks, markers, and poster board or whatever method you choose for mounting. Visit the dollar store for these things.

- Food is a good idea. Serve food and drinks at the beginning when people gather and as you move into the teaching time. If you have food for the second half of the event, stick to clean and simple finger foods. You don't want spills or greasy fingers on the vision boards.

- Choose music selections. Piano, soft jazz, classical, worship music … what will set the mood for creativity? Do you want an upbeat and fun environment or a contemplative mood? The right music will help achieve the tone you want.

PROMOTE

- Make your invitation list.
- Decide how you will send invitations: text, call, evite, or mailed paper invitation.
- If you are a coach or women's ministry coordinator and you have an unlimited number of people to whom you are announcing this event, you will need to decide upon the announcement and registration process. This is important for an organized and smooth event.
- Consider expanding your guest list by giving gifts to those who bring a friend (ideas: church swag like a T-shirt, a coupon for a free coffee from the church café, a discount for the women's retreat). It is not about the gift as much as it is about the enthusiasm. People simply love to win things because it is fun!
- Follow up with people to obtain RSVPs. (Don't be surprised at the turnout. Be prepared!)
- Keep your guests excited about the event with friendly and motivating quotes and messages via text or Facebook messenger. Consider making a video message if you are a coach or a women's ministry coordinator. Don't let attendees forget about this!

PLAYTIME!

It's time for your event!

While this can simply be a workshop of cutting and pasting and then sharing in small groups, consider beginning with a bit of teaching. Testimonials about God's faithfulness and provision are exciting because we tend respond to the emotional and spiritual appeal of one another's stories.

Remember the key point of chapter three about the Law of Attraction? It is an unbiblical practice and it has invaded our culture and the way we think. A bit of teaching is recommended to frame the concept of vision boards in a biblical way.

A suggested outline follows for a two-hour event. It is designed for a group of approximately fifteen to twenty. Modifications can easily be made for a smaller or larger group. Pay attention to the intention of the outline and make adjustments as needed to fit your needs. Note the additional supplies suggested in the outline. God bless you and your event participants!

EVENT OUTLINE

Objective

Participants would understand the biblical concept of a vision and the use of a vision board. Participants would create a vision board during the workshop.

Greet

Before the event, prepare name tags by writing a number on each one. Prior registration will come in handy at this point. Don't use numbers higher than the number of people expected. Then prepare slips of paper with instructions such as:

Introduce #4 to #12.
Find out #7's favorite beverage.
Ask #5 and #13 if they prefer dogs or cats.

When attendees arrive, welcome them with a name tag and slip of paper, then they can head into the main room to get refreshments and mill about to meet people and complete their assignment. The purpose of this mixer is to set a tone of fun, to establish the hands-on nature of the event, and to start developing relationships.

Opening Words

We're glad you're here today, and I suppose you are here because you have something you want to accomplish or you want a new approach to life. Did you know that 92 percent of New Year's goals fail by mid-January? Yet year after year, people set goals. Why? Because Ecclesiastes 3:11 says God makes everything beautiful in its time and he has placed eternity in our hearts. We are designed to move forward, improve, grow, and prepare for more. Even though growing and achieving are hard to do, on some level, we want the challenge. Don't throw in the towel now that you've heard this statistic! What you will learn today will drastically improve your results.

More than achieving goals, most people want a life of purpose and joy. Most people want the satisfaction of knowing they are doing what they are meant to do. You may know several people who are truly happy and exude confidence in their lives. These people are often successful in their lives and careers because they are doing "what they were made to do."

(Insert a very brief story of someone you know like this. For instance, I would share about my chiropractor who loves serving people, believes in chiropractic, has a waiting room full of patients every time I am there, and makes a positive impact in the community through winter coat drives and toy donations at Christmastime.)

It is infectious being around people who are like this!

To achieve goals—or the kind of life we dream of—writing goals makes the difference. We give ourselves a 50 percent greater chance if we write down our goals. Thinking about it is good, but putting ideas into a logical statement is better, and sharing it with trusted people is better yet. Making a vision board is going to take our ideas up a notch and set the stage for achievement.

Activity

Each one of us came here today with ideas of what we want and what we feel led to do. Around the room are posterboards labeled with vision/goal categories including: physical health, financial (money or career-oriented goals), relational (relationship or family-oriented goals), spiritual (growing closer to God), social, or recreational. I'd like you to walk around the room and find the poster that categorizes your greatest vision. This will give you the opportunity to meet others who have similar goals.

Go around your small group and share your vision, goals, and/ or thoughts on this subject. Write your names on the poster. You'll get back together again later!

(Give participants five minutes for this exercise.)

Testimonial

Prearrange for someone from your group to give a good three- to five-minute testimonial of God's protection, provision, and blessing. People love to hear a touching testimony! It also helps create a setting where participants will share from the heart. They will also think about waiting upon the Lord expectantly regarding their own needs and desires.

Teach objective 1 – Understand the biblical concept of vision and use of vision boards:

So far we've been using terms interchangeably. Let's talk about how everything connects like puzzle pieces.

(Note: Each of the below paragraphs explains a term, and each term could be a visual of a puzzle piece that will fit together.)

Visions occurred often during biblical times. God Himself came to people while waking or sleeping, or he sent angels to reveal His plan for them.

Today, we have God's Word and the Holy Spirit to help us discern. God's will for our lives is much simpler than we often think. God's mission (His will) for our lives is in three parts. That we would know Him personally (salvation), then grow in Him (sanctification), and live with Him forever in heaven (glorification). That's it.

The exact way we fulfill our mission is unique to each one of us. We are all given personalities, life experiences, talents, and opportunities. How we each live out our callings and our life visions is different.

A vibrant walk with the Lord includes our prayerful contemplation and active participation. Through reading the Bible and praying, we can be asking whether our activities, goals, and desires are in line with God's will for us.

When we are considering our visions and creating goals to support our visions, we can surrender them to God. We can ask in prayer if we are growing closer toward or moving farther from the Lord.

Where do our trust and dependence lie?

Do we trust in our wisdom, our abilities, our strength, our resources ... or the Lord's?

1) Our intelligence is found in His ultimate wisdom.

2) Our inadequacies are perfected in His sufficiency.

3) Our weakness is His strength.

4) Our lack is His abundance.

Activity

At your table, you will find a folded tent card with questions to discuss. We'll take ten minutes for this.

(Note: Prepare sheets ahead of time with the following discussion questions.)

Second Chronicles 16:9 says, "For the eyes of the Lord move to and fro throughout the earth that He may strongly support those whose heart is completely His." If I allow the Lord to strongly support me, what may occur in my life? What may come of my vision?

Psalm 127:1 says, "Unless the Lord builds the house, the laborer labors in vain." What could our lives look like if everything we are living for is of God?

Do I trust in my wisdom, abilities, strength, and resources ... or the Lord's?

Teach objective 2 — Participants will create a vision board:

Before we start cutting out magazine pictures, I hope our discussion has been informing your thoughts and refining your vision.

Vision boards are often misunderstood. We hear people talk of things materializing in their life through the Law of Attraction, but this is an over-spiritualization of the way the brain operates. And this gives credit to humans, while taking the glory away from God, the giver of all good gifts.

By posting pictures of what we desire, how we want to live, and what we are working toward, we are increasing the likelihood of it coming to pass. We are helping the brain create a new string of thoughts, otherwise known as building memories. This makes achievement of something new seem normal and, therefore, possible.

As we refer to and look at our vision board, it can be a tool for prayer. That said, we ought to be careful to not focus our thoughts on things more than we delight in the Creator. We cannot manipulate God to do what we want. Nor do we want to fall into a formulaic faith such as "five easy steps to successful living."

Take the vision board for what it is, a creative project to focus our thoughts, goals, and desires and to live on purpose. The vision board can assist our prayer life and it can be an aid to create new habits, transform thoughts, and live to one's potential.

Let's take thirty to forty-five minutes to make our vision boards now! Have fun! I will let you know when we have ten minutes left so you can pace yourself.

Activity

After the vision board creation time has passed, a powerful time comes in sharing the vision board in a small group.

- Have the small groups reconvene to share. From these conversations come authentic moments, including laughter and tears, accountability, and new friendships. Each small group may have about fifteen minutes for heartfelt conversation.

- Encourage attendees to exchange contact information with at least one person in their group for accountability and encouragement in the days ahead.

- End with a large-group prayer of dedication.

- Encourage teams to pose for a group picture.

- Dial it up a notch by taking each woman's picture holding her vision board and each small group's picture.

- Send pictures to each woman's cell phone the following day with a message such as

Today is the first day living by your vision.
Seize the day!

ᏹ

BONUS GUIDE #2

What to Post on a Vision Board

Look for and cut out pictures, words, fonts, and colors that inspire. A picture is worth a thousand words!

What evokes the ideals tucked away in my heart?

Consider including elements from the following areas of life:

- Financial
- Spiritual
- Intellectual
- Relational
- Physical health
- Vocational
- Recreational

How do I aspire to care for my soul?

How do I want to grow as a Christ follower?

What character traits do I want to strengthen?

What natural talents and abilities do I want to develop into true strengths?

What knowledge do I want to attain? How will I aspire toward mastery? Include serving opportunities, mission trips, ministries, and charities to support.

What do I want to celebrate

- a year from now?
- two years from now?
- in five years?
- in ten years?

What might I regret later in life if I don't pursue it now?

Bucket list items: How do I want to experience life?

Wish list items: What do I currently want and need?

Achievements and completed milestones bring a great feeling of satisfaction.

- What do I want to stretch myself to accomplish?
- What breakthrough do I want to experience?
- What do I want to elevate?

Money is a tool.

- How do I want to work with it?
- What might I want to learn in the category of finances?
- How do I want to earn, save, spend, and share it?

Relationships:

- What kind of woman do I want to be in my most important relationships?
- How do I want my friends and loved ones to describe me?
- How do I want to contribute toward their lives?

What do I think God is calling me to?

Brainstorm Ideas for My BHAG

– my big holy audacious goal

About the Author

JULIE STROUD, ACC, is a business coach and owner of Fervent Coaching. Christian coaching for entrepreneurial women, Fervent Coaching exists to inspire and educate women to live their unique calling. Julie does this through writing, speaking, and coaching. The vision of Fervent Coaching is for every woman to use her gifts for the glory of God. For information about Vision Board events for Christian women, coaching programs, webinars, or to have Julie speak for your group, visit www.ferventcoaching.com.

Join Us!

Join the community of women just like you who are living all-in. Trusting God and living your unique calling is a faith-on-fire kind of life. Christian entrepreneurial sister, we need each other!

Fervent means intensity of spirit, enthusiastic, hot, and glowing. Really… is there any other way to live and work?

Share a picture of your vision board and post your vision board stories at **#FerventVisionBoard**. Through this hashtag, you can share, rejoice, ask questions, engage, and participate in our online events.

Finally, mark your calendar for the second Saturday of January, National Vision Board Day. We host an online vision board event on that special day! Keep posted at **#FerventVisionBoard**.